Contents

People of
ZIONSBORG

Written & Compiled by
DOUG & SANDY ALVSTAD

A special thanks to families who provided stories and photos, the Evansville Historical Foundation, Douglas County Historical Society, Grant County Historical museum, and Tami Erickson.

Contents

People of
ZIONSBORG

A Short History of Zionsborg Lutheran Church

On December of 1884 Zionsborg Church was born (Swedish Evangelical Lutheran). Land for the church building and cemetery was donated by Ole Alberts, who served as the church's first treasurer. The first officers were Deacons-Nils Alldrin, Erik Nelson, and Johann O. Peterson; Trustees-Erik Malmgren, Ole Alberts and Peter Erickson; Secretary- Peter Alldrin. Among the forty-eight charter members were Mr. and Mrs. John Lindstrom and Fritz; Mr. and Mrs. Peter Setterlund and Ann;, Ole Erickson; Mr. and Mrs. John Peterson, Frank and Martin; Peter J. Peterson; Mr. and Mrs. Ole Peterson; Mr. and Mrs. Erik Nelson, John and Emily; Mr. and Mrs. Erick Malmgren; Mr. and Mrs. Per Erickson, Albin; Mr. and Mrs. Nils Nilson Frykman; and Mr. and Mrs. Ole Alberts. Within a year, the first church was built. Built on a hill, Zionsborg probably was named because "Zion" originally meant hill and "New Zion" referred to heaven -"borg" means fortress. Perhaps, to the settlers of this area Zionsborg was a spiritual fortress.

The Rev. Kronberg was the first minister as Zionsborg was aligned with Christina Lake. Realignment occurred in 1890 with Wennersborg and Fyksande. In 1898, a Swedish School began (unknown how long it lasted) and a horse barn just south of the road was erected to house horses of the church members. Other realignments occurred as the call for pastors was needed.

In 1914, English was used in the service. June 24, 1917, a fire broke out from lightning striking the building and destroyed the original church. A new church was built on that spot and completed October 8, 1919.

In 1965, it became apparent that the church was no longer sustainable with fewer people in the area. The doors were closed and most of the building was sold off with some paintings, religious objects, etc. donated to Immanuel church in Evansville and the pulpit eventually ended up in the Evansville Historical Foundation.

The following biographies are alphabetical by last name, but are in family groups when possible. Names in bold have grave sites at Zionsborg Cemetery and included in this book if they passed prior to February 2014.

Ole Albert(s) Family Home Page

In 1866, Ole came to Minnesota looking for farm land. He purchased 212 acres in Evansville township and set up homestead on the south shore of what is now Lake Albert. He returned to Wisconsin, and married **Oline** Peterson in 1874 in Madison, Wisconsin. Then he and his bride returned to Minnesota. In 1876, Oline gave birth to twin boys, who died in infancy. (Although there are no grave markers on the farm or on the cemetery, it is thought that it is possible the twins were buried on the Albert's lot in Zionsborg Cemetery since there is a burial space between Ole's and Oline's headstone. It was common in those days for parents to be buried on either side of an infant or infants in what was called "cradling." In 1884, Ole and Oline donated the plot of land on which the Zionsborg church and cemetery was established. Ole and Olin were charter members of Zionsborg church and Ole was the first treasurer.

Log cabin still standing in 2012

View of Lake Albert from the homestead

Ole and Oline Albert(s)

Ole Albert (also spelled Alberts) was born in Solor, Norway in 1839. He immigrated to American and lived in Dane County, Wisconsin until he volunteered to the Wisconsin 12th regiment, Company G in November of 1861. His "... regiment, known as the 'Marching Twelfth,' was organized in Oct., 1861, at Camp Randall and left the state Jan. 11, 1862 ...It was sent to Columbus Ky., to repair railroads and rebuild bridges and from there to Humboldt, Tenn., from which point it made numerous brilliant expeditions, clearing the country of guerrillas and bridge-burners. In the fall of 1862 it was sent south with the Army of the Mississippi engaging in numerous skirmishes, notably at Hernando, Miss., and the Coldwater River. It was engaged in the investment of Vicksburg, with small loss; was at the second battle of Jackson, and at Big Shanty where it charged 2 miles through the timber, capturing the first skirmish line of the enemy. ...Joining in the march to the sea, it assisted in the investment of Savannah and the Carolina campaign...joined the triumphant march north through Petersburg, Richmond, Fredericksburg and Alexandria, participated in the grand review at Washington, and was mustered out at Louisville, July 16, 1865." (*The Union Army*, vol. 4, p. 52) and he was mustered out in July of 1865.

Ole and Oline raised 5 sons and 3 daughters: Susie Alberts Nelson, Adolph, Theodore, Otto, Ella Alberts Gilbertson, Robert, Oscar and Francis. Robert Alberts was the only member of the family to remain in Douglas County. Buried at Zionsborg are **Ole, Oline, Oscar, Robert (Clarence), Susie Nelson, Francis, Frances, Ida, Otto, and Denise.** As you read the individual family pages, you will see that church, music, and education must have been strongly encouraged in the Albert family.

They continued to farm and raise children until Ole's death in 1909. Ole died of an apparent heart attack. "He left about one o'clock Sunday telling his wife that he was going to call on Ole C. Nelson, who lived a mile distant...four hours later he was found by the roadside face downward, by Clarence Nelson and J E. Gillis, the latter a neighbor. The attack had evidently been brought on through overexertion in walking. He was a very large man and had had no exercise the past winter." (*Alexandria Post News*, 6 May 1909, p7col2) He died May 2, 1909.

Oline Albert

Oline Peterson was born near Bergen, Norway, April 15, 1854. In 1861 she came to America with her parents who settled near Madison. In July 16, 1874 or 1873, **Ole Albert** and Oline were married. They returned to the homestead in Minnesota, where they had ten children. According to the Grant County Herald, June 6, 1929, they had twelve children. "Four died in infancy and three later in life." But at this time we have no record of 12.

Ole and Oline donated land for the Zionsborg Church and Cemetery in which all could be buried who so desired whether member or not. She and her husband were charter members.

Oline lived on the farm until 1914; then she moved to Elbow Lake and lived with her daughter **Susie** and her husband **John E. Nelson**. She died May 30, 1929. Her funeral services were held at the J.E. Nelson home and at the Zionsborg church. Reverend Carl A.E. Gustafson read at the home and "his sermon at the church was in English." Interestingly, the obituary says that "Rev. Peterson of Evansville spoke in Swedish" (eventhough,The Alberts were Norwegian!) "Her pall bearers were J.E. Gillies, **Adolph Solberg**, Olof and Nils Setterlund and A.V. and **Oscar Malmgren**.

"Among those present from away for the funeral were **Otto B. Alberts** of Los Angeles, Mrs. George [Ella] Gilbertson of Duluth, and Mr. and Mrs. Oscar Normann and daughter of Ole Normann of Fergus Falls, Mrs. A.E. Nelson of Barnesville, and Mr. and Mrs. Cornelius Bergeson, Mr. and Mrs. Palmer Bergeson, and Miss Lena Erickson of Duluth."

Ole and Oline's children included twin boys who died in 1876, Adolph, Theodore, **Otto, Oscar, Robert** (Clarence), **Susie**, Ella, and **Frances**.

Frances Genevieve Alberts

According to the *Grant County Herald* May 3, 1923, "Frances Genevieve Alberts died Monday, April 30 at 5:30 p.m. at St. Raphael's Hospital, St. Cloud, from pneumonia. Miss Alberts, who is a daughter of Mrs. **Olina Alberts** of Elbow lake, had been employed in the Guy Photo shop at St. Cloud as bookkeeper. Several weeks ago she had an attack of 'flu,' apparently recovered and returned to work again She was taken ill again Friday, April 20, and was taken to the hospital where her doctors...pronounced the ailment double pneumonia. ..

Frances Genevieve Alberts was born at Evansville, May 16, 1895. In 1911 she came to Elbow Lake to attend high school and since that time has made her home with her sister, Mrs. J.E. Nelson. She graduated from Elbow lake High School in 1914. In 1915 she received a graduate certificate from the teacher training department of the high school and during the next six years taught school. She taught near Elbow Lake for two years, near Fergus Falls two years, at Wendell one year, and at Leonard one year. She took a business course in the College of Commerce at St. Cloud last year. During the past three months she has been employed in the Guy Studio in St. Cloud.

She was a member of the Zionsborg church near Evansville and also a member of the Eastern Star lodge..."

Oscar Alberts

Oscar Eugene Alberts , son of **Ole and Oline Alberts**, was born November 14, 1892 and died October 11, 1902. Young Oscar died of appendicitis when he was only 10 years old.

Otto Alberts

"Masonic funeral services for Otto Alberts, 86, a former Evansville area resident, were held Wednesday at Erickson Funeral home, Elbow Lake. Burial was at Zionsborg cemetery, Evansville. Mr. Alberts died Saturday at Santa Monica, Calif.

Organist was Mrs. Harold Mohagen. Pallbeareres were James Strand, F.C.Mattson, Anthon Huseth, Arnold Johnson, David Norholm and James Gingerich.

Mr. Alberts was born Sept. 11 1885 at Evansville. [Actually he was born on the Alberts homestead in Evansville Township **to Ole and Oline Alberts.**] He worked as a carpenter 40 years before retiring. [He died June 24, 1972]

He is survived by four nieces and three nephews, Mrs. Walter (Irene) Baldwin and Mrs. Glen (Beulah) Olson, Evansville; **Denise Alberts**, Santa Monica, Calif.; Mrs. Marian Agre, Duluth; Edmond Gilbertson, Pasadena, Calif.; **Francis Alberts**, Colton, Calif., and Eugene Alberts, Elbow Lake." *Grant County Herald*, June 29, 1972.

(Clarence) Robert Alberts

Born **Clarence Robert Alberts**, Robert was born to Ole and Oline Albert, March 13, 1890. According to the Albert Family history, he grew up on the Ole Albert homestead and attended school in District #26 (see map) along with his brothers and sisters. One of the family stories told that Robert and a neighbor boy "were kept after school as punishment

for some misdemeanor. Soon after dismissal time, threatening clouds in the western sky indicated a storm was approaching. The boys recognized the fear in the voice of the teacher as he offered to release them earlier than she had planned. Realizing that her offer was prompted by her wish to leave the schoolhouse and get to her boarding place before the storm broke, the boys decided to decline the offer. With the storm nearly upon them, they suddenly dashed out the door and high tailed it for home, leaving the frightened teacher alone with no time to reach her boarding place before the storm hit.

As a young man, he and his brothers Adolph, Theodore and Otto ran "a steam threshing rig with which they did custom threshing in the western and central parts of Douglas County." When his father died in 1909, Robert returned home from Northwestern College in Fergus Falls, MN to help his youngest brother Theodore run the farm.

He married **Ida** Roswold on November 17, 1913. On the Ole Albert homestead they raised four children: **Denise**, Irene, Beulah, and **Francis**. "Robert and Ida's love of music was passed on to their children. Many songs were taught as Robert sang to the girls while he sat milking the cows in the evening.

Robert died December 16, 1927 at the young age of 37 of tuberculosis. David Thompson, Irene's son, recalls his mother telling him that when Robert left for St. Cloud to be treated there, he called each of the children to his side and told them what they were to do to help their mother. Irene believed he knew he would not be returning.

Ida Alberts

Ida was born to Sivert and Inger Roswold February 17, 1887, In Urness township. She married **Robert Alberts** November 17, 1913. According to the *Lake Region Press,* September 1, 1971, "Most of her life was spent in the Evansville area, but for a number of years in her later life she

(LtoR) Irene Alberts Thompson Baldwin, Francis Alberts, Ida
Roswold Alberts, Beulah Alberts Olson, and Denise Alberts

made her home with a daughter, Denise in Santa Monica, Calif. For the past year and a half she had been a resident of Crestview Manor Nursing Home at Evansville." At the time of her death, she was survived by her 4 children: Irene Baldwin, Bula Olson (Glen), **Denise Alberts**, and **Francis Alberts**...also her sister Ricka (Mrs. C.J. Richards) of Monrovia, CA and a brother Albert of Evansville. She was preceded in death by her parents, two brothers, three sisters, and her husband.

Her funeral service was held at "Immanuel Lutheran Church in Evansville on Friday, July 30 with Pastor Lorance O. Schoenberg officiating. Mrs. Ragnar Listrom church organist accompanied Dennis and David Thompson (Irene's sons) who sang "Children of the Heavenly Father." Pallbearers were five grandsons, Bruce, Roger and Mark Olson, Dennis and David Thompson and nephew Orville Roswold." Ida died July 27, 1971, at the Douglas County Hospital.

Denise Alberts

Born **Opal Denise Alberts**, Denise was born to **Robert and Ida Alberts**, May 22, 1916. She grew up on the **Ole Albert** homestead and attended school in district #26 along with her brothers and sisters. We know that she was still at home in 1930 according to the Census. However, at some time after that, she became a teacher and moved to California. In 1960, her home address was Santa Monica. According to her obituary, Denise Alberts, resident of in Mar Vista, California, died at the age of 68, November 25, 1984 at St. Joseph's Hospital in Phoenix, Arizona. However, the social security death index has her death listed in Los Angeles, California.

Her funeral was held at the Erickson Funeral Home in Elbow Lake with Reverend Merle Fagerberg officiating. Mrs. Renee (Harold) Mohagen played the organ, and her casket bearers were Bruce, Mark, and Roger Olson, David and Dennis Thompson and Orville Roswold. At the time of her death, she was survived by two sisters—Irene (Thompson) Baldwin and Beulah Olson—and one brother **Francis Alberts**.

Francis Alberts

Francis Robert Alberts was born August 8, 1924, **to Robert and Ida Alberts**. "He was baptized and confirmed at Immanuel Lutheran Church in Evansville, Francis graduated from Evansville High School and then entered into the United States Air Force, serving in World war II, from September 13, 1943 to November 6, 1945. After service, Francis was employed as an operating engineer of heavy equipment in California. He retired in 1986. Francis spent his winters in California and his summers in Evansville.

He is survived by his two daughters, Cindy Alberts of Portland, Oregon, and Ginny (Bruce) MacDonald, of Whittier, California; two grandsons Ian and Brett MacDonald; two sisters, Irene Baldwin and Beula Olson, both of Alexandria, Minnesota, and many nieces and nephews. He was preceded in death by his parents and one sister." Erickson-Smith Obituary

"Cpl. Francis R. Alberts, Eight Air Force, writes his mother, Ida Alberts of Evanville, he arrived in England. His letter, in part: "I had a good Xmas day; we had turkey and all that goes with it. We are now at our base and it is real place. All our crew stays in the same barrack which makes it nice. This afternoon we played football, went to a show and saw Deanna Durbin in 'Christmas Holiday'... [he] received training at Amarillo, TX, Sioux Falls, SD, Yuma, AZ, and Sioux City, IA." News article, Thursday, January 18, 1945.

Francis passed away at the Douglas County Hospital in Alexandria

May 14, 1994. His funeral was held at Faith Lutheran Church in Evansville May 17, 1994 with Rev. Irv Arnquist and Rev. George Larson officiating. His sister Irene was the organist and his nephews David and Dennis sang two duets, "Great is Thy Faithfulness" and "Peace like a River." Pallbearers were Dennis and David Thompson, Mark and Bruce Olson, Dennis Nelson, and Earl Erickson.

Aldrin Home Page

Nils Aldrin or Nels was born in Sweden in 1847 and immigrated to the US in 1868 (according to the 1910 Census). He set up homestead February 20, 1877, on 177.16 acres in Urness Township 128 Section 6 just south of Zionsborg Church. Also found on plat maps of Erdahl township section 32 in Grant County is a 160 acre piece in Nels Aldrin's name. In 1894, he married **Mary** Schroder daughter of Kirstie Schroder or Schoeder, widow who had 7 children. He and Mary had one child Freda born in 1896. (Freda later married Odell Johnson, and they had only one child Fern Marion.) Later Urness plat maps indicate that Freda owned the homestead and the 160 acres in Erdahl township. Unknown at this time how Nils Aldrin and Olof Alldrin were related. Nils along with **Erik Nelson** and **Johann O. Peterson** was elected as deacon of the first organization of Zionsborg Church. Below is a picture of Freda's wedding dress at the Evansville Historical Foundation and map of the area Aldrin's came from.

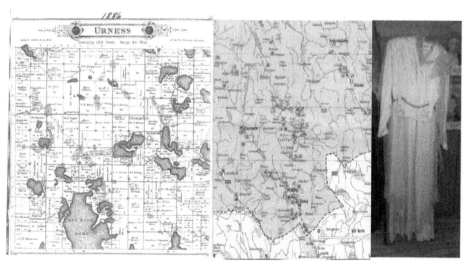

Nels and Mary Aldrin

Nels Aldrin (also spelled Nils Alldrin) was born in Sweden in 1847 and

immigrated to the US in 1868 (according to the 1910 Census). He set up homestead Feb. 20, 1877, on 177.16 acres in Urness township 128 Section 6 just south of Zionsborg Church. Also found on plat maps of Erdahl township section 32 in Grant County is a 160 acre piece in the Nils Aldrin name.

According to Tore Bakken, Swedish researcher, Anders Alldrin (birth date unknown) and his wife Marit Markusdougther born June 1, 1810, had two children, Anders Alldrin born Sep.23 1843 and Nils Alldrin born Aug. 24 1845. This Nils was the one who worked for Olof Alldrin in Sweden. (see Alldrin home page). He also found Anders Alldrin's wife Marit Markusdougther married a second time to Olof Mattsson born Feb.3, 1831. Marit and had two more children. Lena Olofsdougther born Mars 18, 1851, and Christina Olofsdougther born Okt.12 1853.

According to **Gladys Gerhardt's** family history, Nels Aldrin was a friend of **John Johnson** and Nels's half-sister was Lena (Mattson) Lundblad. With encouragement from Nels, John sent for Lena in 1887 and married her.

Nels was married in 1894 to **Mary** Schroder and had only one child Freda born in 1896. (Freda later married Odell Johnson, and they had only one child Fern Marion

He died December 23, 1912. (No obituary was found in Douglas County, Evansville, or Grant County Historical Societies.) Nels may have been a nephew or cousin to Olof Alldrin since they lived in one area of Sweden and worked together.

Mary Aldrin

Mary (daughter of Kirstie Schroeder, widow, according to the US Census) (perhaps of Olof Johnsson and Kirstin Nilsdotter from Varmland Sweden) was born October 25, 1857, and immigrated in 1881 from Sweden. Her siblings included Jan Jacob, Erik Johan (John), Nils F., Carolina, Anna Maria Schroeder, and Lars Johan Olson. She was married in 1894 to **Nils Aldrin** and had only one child Freda born in 1896 when she was 39 and Nils was 49. Her mother Kirstie lived with them on the farm near Zionsborg for some time. Her brother John moved to Souris,ND and was one of the builders and earliest deacons of the Swedish Zion Lutheran Church, known as the Stone Church near Souris. (Wunderlich, Gene. *Stone Church, a Prairie Parable*. 2012)

According the *Evansville Enterprise*, December 26, 1935, "Mrs. Mary Aldrin, nee Schroeder was born October 25, 1847, in Fryksande, Vermlands lan, Sweden, and died Wednesday morning, the 18th at the Douglas County Hospital, at the age of 78, 1 months and 23 days...

Since Mr. Aldrin died in 1912 she has made her home in Evansville, mostly. She was a member of the Zionsborg Lutheran Church since 1894, but since coming to Evansville the local Immanuel congregation was largely her church home. Aldrin has enjoyed fair health, even at her age, and it was only about ten days before her death that more alarming symptoms occurred. Her going, therefore, was quite unexpected, as it's often the case with death...

Funeral services were held at the iZonsborg [sic] Lutheran Church on Saturday afternoon. .. Miss Alice Frykman sang: 'Till friden hem, till ratta fadershusetmin trotta sial med rangtan stracker sig,' a Swedish song which was dear to the departed...She was laid to rest in the church cemetery beside her husband, to await that wonderful day 'When Jesus Comes in Glory.'

Those most deeply mourning her departure are Mr. and Mrs. Odell Johnson, her son in law and daughter; a little granddaughter, Fern Marion; a brother, John Schroeder, Souris, N.D; and a sister Mrs. Olof Nordstrom, Big Timber Montana..."

Alldrin Home Page

Olof Alldrin was born in Varmsland, Sweden, August 29, 1825. He immigrated to America June 12, 1868, on the ship *City of New York* along with **Maria Ersdotter** and 4 children: Anders Gustaf, Amelia, Alf, and Oscar (from the passenger list of the *City of New York* Ancestry.com). June 5, 1872 Olof bought 183.7 acres in Urness Township and July 1, 1874, he bought another 160 (in sections 6 and 7). There are three Olof Alldrins. Olof's son and then his grandson carries the name Ole, which creates some confusion when researching.

(from Tore Bakken bakkentorsby@telia.com, a researcher in Sweden) he found a lot of Alldrins in Fryksände parish (Torsby) just south from Torsby on the countryside in SVENNEBY. "Olof Alldrin had a lot of farmerhands and maidens on his farm.There was a farmerhand Nils Alldrin born Aug.24 1845 working on the farm. In Westanvik Torsby where

Tore Bakken lives - lived Karl Alldrin and his wife Karin Persdougther and children: Maria Alldrin born Dec.14 1851 and Per Alldrin born Now. 19 1853." Per, or Peter, was one of the founding fathers of Zionsborg. His mother and one sister Carrie are buried in Kensington, and Peter and family moved to California.

(Evansville Historical Society)

Olof and Maria Alldrin

Olof Alldrin was born in Varmsland, Sweden, August 29, 1825. He immigrated to America, June 12, 1868, on the ship *City of New York* along with **Maria Ersdotter** and 4 children: Anders Gustaf, Amelia, Alf , and Oscar (from the passenger list of the *City of New York*). June 5, 1872 Olof bought 183.7 acres in Urness Township and July 1, 1874, he bought another 160 (in sections 6 and 7)The 1875 census shows they live in Urness township with Ole, Gustaf, Emelie, Alfred and Oscar. In the 1885 census Olof and family live in Urness. However, the 1880 census showed him living in Evansville with his son Ole, Ole's wife Kate (Borgen) and their child. Maria was listed in the 1880 census living on the farm with Gust, Alfred, and Oskar). Olof listed his occupation as hardware merchant. He died July 5, 1893.

According to the *Evansville Enterprise* July 7, 1893, "Gust and Ole Alldrin were called to Fergus Falls on Wednesday by the sickness of their father.

LATER.—Mr. Olof Alldrin died at the residence of his son in Fergus

Falls on Wednesday Evening. He was in his 67th year. The body was taken to this place, from which it was conveyed to his son, Ole Alldrin's place. The funeral takes place to-day (Friday) the remains will be laid to rest in the cemetery by the church near Chippewa mills. Mr. Alldrin was one of the best known settlers in this vicinity, and has always enjoyed the confidence and respect of all who knew him." Note- Karl and Olof Alldrin were brothers.   Karin was married to Karl, she immigrated in 1874 and he registered as a naturalized citizen sometime in 1869-1873. His wife was a widow by 1877 and living between Olof and Nels. In 1875 census she is listed with Peter her son, who immigrated in 1870. Peter, a cousin of Gladys Johnson Rohloff Gerhardt, was an original trustee of Zionsborg and later moved to California. Karin is buried in Kensington as is Carrie Alldrin, sister of Christina Hovde (Halvor), who also immigrated in 1874.

Maria Alldrin

Maria Alldrin was born Ersdotter in Sweden, April 21, 1826. She and Olof were married 27 Dec, 1846, in Fryksande, Varmland. Her parents were Erik Johsson and Marit Nilsdotter. She was a sister to **Per "Peter" Erickson**. (Information from Bonne Erickson) She immigrated to the US, June 12, 1868, on the ship *City of New York* along with **Olof** and 4 children: Anders Gustaf, Amelia, Alf, and Oscar (from the passenger list of the *City of New York*. [no Ole] In 1875 she lived in Urness township with Ole, Gustaf, Emelie, Alfred and Oscar. The 1885 census listed her and Olof in Urness Township with Gustaf, Amelia, and Oscar.

She died August 14, 1896. According to her obituary, "Mrs. Maria Aldrin, well known to all the old residents in this neighborhood, died at the residence of her daughter, Mrs. Emma Thorsen, at Fergus Falls, last Friday Aug. 14, at the old age of seventy years. She was the mother of Ole, Gustav, and Oscar Aldrin, Mrs. Emma Thorsen, and aunt to Mrs. Nels Eckblad..." [unknown at this time who Mrs. Nels Ekblad was.)

Alvstad Home Page

The Carl Alvstad family moved in 1947 from a farm near Ashby after buying the Bristol farm on the Chippewa River. This was the site of the Chippewa Mill (AKA the Meeker Mill). Zionsborg Cemetery burial lot includes Carl Tillman Alvstad and his wife Amelia Augusta (Abel), their son Gary Alvstad, their son Leslie Alvstad and wife Karen (Ray), and son Douglas and wife Sandra (nee Bellamy . Brokhausen). Sandra's mother **Mary Louise Brokhausen** is to be buried in a lot nearby.

Original homestead home   Home built in 1969

Carl and Amelia Alvstad

Carl Tillman Alvstad was born April 23, 1911, in Fergus Falls, Minnesota, to Eric and Mina Alvstad of rural Ashby. He was the second born in a family of 5 girls and 3 boys (Grace, Mae, Edna, Ellen, Lillian, Carl, Marcus, and Lyle. He grew up on the family farm in Pelican Lake Township and attended rural School District #9, where he graduated from eighth grade.

Carl married **Amelia** Abel of Hoffman, Minnesota, on August 23, 1942. They were the parents of three boys-- Leslie, **Gary** and Douglas. Carl started his farming career about two miles east of Pomme de Terre Lake. In February of 1947 he purchased and moved his family to a farm about 2/3 mile west of Zionsborg on Douglas County Road 54/56. Like most farmers in the late 40's and 50's Carl ran a diversified farm, milking Holstein cows, and also raising pigs, chickens, ducks and geese. Along with the garden produce, it was a rigorous but rewarding life style.

Carl enjoyed trapping and life along the Chippewa River. Numerous mink, muskrat, raccoon and fox pelts helped pay debts and made way for more presents under the Christmas tree during the holiday season. He could play the guitar and harmonica, and family get-togethers with

14

his brothers and sisters could be real hoot. Each of his 5 sisters could play the piano and the two brothers also played guitar. A brother-law, Morris Strom played the fiddle, so family gatherings could break out into joyous music.

Carl had an unfortunate accident when he was about 35 years old when pounding on some metal a sliver broke off and got caught in his right eye causing the loss of vision. A few years later his eye was removed, and he received one of the first glass eye operations in the state of Minnesota. He seldom complained, and his three sons seldom gave thought to the realization that their dad was blind in one eye because he seemed so normal.

Carl retired from milking at age 65 and raised a small herd of beef cattle his last years on the farm. He gave up trapping at 84 mainly because his wife didn't trust his footing on the slippery river backs at that age. In the fall of 1997 he moved to the North Star Manor in Hoffman. He entered the Good Samaritan Nursing Home in the fall of 1999. His health rapidly diminished. In his last two years, he was unable to walk or interact with his family. He passed away February 19, 2003, at the age of 91.

Amelia Alvstad

"Amelia Augusta Abel Alvstad passed away Sunday, January 26, 2014, at the Evansville Care Campus. Amelia was born August 16, 1920, to William and Louise (Lorenz) Abel at Hoffman, Minnesota. She was the tenth of the twelve Abel children and was named after both of her grandmothers. She

15

was baptized and confirmed at Zion Lutheran Church in Hoffman and graduated from Hoffman High School.

Amelia was married to Carl Alvstad, August 23, 1942, making their first home in Pomme de Terre Township. They purchased their family farm in Elk Lake Township in 1947. Three sons were born to them-- Leslie, Gary, and Douglas. Amelia spent her life as a farm woman, doing everything from milking cows to hauling bales. She loved being outdoors. She was active in all of the churches where she belonged as an adult, which were Zionsborg, Lincoln, and Messiah, serving as a women's group officer, and serving faithfully in the kitchen for many

Alvstad family 1946

events. She was a member of the Zionsborg Cemetery Association and always enjoyed the annual meeting and getting together with old friends. She loved watching her grandchildren grow up and especially enjoyed having them stay in her home. The grandchildren fondly remember picking raspberries and tulips, making collages with scraps she'd saved, eating sugared cereal and homemade pudding pops, reenacting fairy tales, playing games and being allowed to drive the pick-up, tractor and mower. She also enjoyed making quilts and afghans for children and grandchildren.

Amelia and Carl moved from their beloved farm in 1998 to the North Star Manor in Hoffman. A few years later, she followed Carl into the Good Samaritan Home in Hoffman where she lived for 13 1/2 years before it closed. She transferred to the Evansville Care Campus in November of 2013.

Amelia is survived by her sons Leslie (Karen), Barrett, and Douglas (Sandra) Alvstad, Evansville; seven grandchildren—Jonathan Alvstad (Tami Erickson), Jennifer (Mike) McLaughlin, Joel (Laura) Alvstad, Janelle (Neil) Mattson, Allison (Nick) Hansen, Brian Alvstad, and Kristina Amundson; fifteen great grandchildren; a sister, Esther Johnson of Barrett, one brother-in-law, Marcus Alvstad, Evansville, and four sisters-in- law—Mae Wick, Edna Strom, Vernie Alvstad, and Ardis Alvstad. She was preceded in death by her parents, husband Carl, son Gary, three

16

brothers and seven sisters" (family submitted obituary)

Gary Alvstad

Gary Dean Alvstad was born December 8, 1944, in Fergus Falls, Minnesota. He was the second of three sons born to **Carl and Amelia Alvstad** of rural Evansville, Minnesota. His brothers were Leslie and Douglas. Gary was baptized at the Pelican Lake Lutheran Church of Ashby and was a confirmed member of Zionsborg. The Alvstad family moved from a farm near Ashby to the Meeker Mill site in Grant County.

His family lived about 2/3 of a mile west of Zionsborg Cemetery on the south side of Douglas County Road 56. Gary attended Evansville Public School District 208 for twelve years and graduated with the class of 1962. He then attended Fergus Falls Community College for one quarter.

He loved the outdoors and was particularly fond of hunting and trapping. In his growing up years, Gary helped his parents with traditional farm chores such as feeding chickens, milking cows, cleaning calf pens, bedding livestock and field work like picking rock, plowing, hauling square hay bales, mowing alfalfa and the not so traditional art of picking cucumbers.

Thursday nights in his teenage years were special because it was roller skating night at the Barrett Pavilion Money made by trapping pocket gophers in the summer and muskrat and mink along with cucumber cash made for good clean weekend fun with his brothers and friends.

Gary was working a summer job for Bob Miles a Barrett farmer in the summer of 1963 when his jacket got hooked in the beaters of a silage unloading box. He was taken to the Grant County Hospital in Elbow Lake and then rushed to Fergus Falls Hospital. He passed away at the age of 18

Farm Accident Takes Life of Gary Alvstad

(July 27, 1969).

Victor and Gerda Anderson

Victor Anderson was born in Princeton, Illinois, October 17, 1884, to John P. Anderson and Ollie (Olivia Olofdotter) who both immigrated from Sweden. He had four brothers—Oscar, **Frank**, Hemming and Alvin—and two sisters **Minnie** and Selma or Alma. Besides Wynat Bureau, Illinois, they lived in Medalia, MN and then moved to Erdahl township in 1915. He volunteered for the draft of World War I, September 12, 1918.

Victor married **Gerda Nilsson Frykman**, daughter of **Per Nilsson Frykman and Stina Petterson**, who lived at the next farm south of his. The 1920 Census listed him and Gerda living with her father. In 1923 they had a daughter Lucille.

According to the *Grant County Herald*, May 20, 1954, "Funeral services for Victor Claus Anderson, 70, who died last Wednesday, May 12, at an Alexandria hospital, were held Saturday, May 15, at the Zionsborg Lutheran church. Death came unexpectedly to this well known neighbor living in the Elk Lake and Erdahl area. He was taken ill on a Monday then rushed to the hospital in Alexandria Wednesday when he died....He was confirmed in the Zionsborg Lutheran Church Dec. 5, 1920, and was a deacon and church board member at the time of his death.

In 1919 he married Miss Gerda Maria Frykman. He is survived by his wife and daughter, Mrs. Charles Peterson, five granddaughters and three brothers Henning, Alvin, and Frank. Officiating at the services was Reb. Pastor Laurel Udden. Music was provided by **Preus Frykman**, who sang 'Beyond the Sunset' accompanied by **Mrs. Oliver Fedje** and a trio consisting of **Victor Setterlund**, Mrs. Leonard Anderson and **Mrs. Edwin Rohloff**.

Pall bearers were **Robert Lindstrom, Rudolph Hansen, Merritt Clow, Bertil Frykman, Leif Erickson**, and **Alvin Frykman**...The entire community mourned the passing of this kind neighbor. He died in Alexandria, Minnesota, May 12, 1954.

Gerda (Frykman) Anderson

The *Grant County Herald*, November 1, 1973, "Funeral services for Mrs. **Gerda Anderson**, 93, were held Tuesday at United Lutheran church, Rev. Allen Hagstrom officiating. Burial was in Zionsborg cemetery, Evansville. She died Saturday at the Barrett Nursing home. Pallbearers were **Alvin**

and Bertil Frykman, Arlin and Willard Anderson, Roger Gustafson and Clifford Carlson. She came with her parents to Erhal township in 1882. She was married to Victor Anderson Nov. 19. 1919. They farmed in Erdahl township. Her husband preceded her in death in 1954. In 1956 (or 1958 hard to read) she moved into Elbow Lake.

She is survived by one daughter, Mrs. Charles (Lucille)Peterson, Cannon Falls, six granddaughters and two great grandchildren. She was also preceded in death by her parents, two sisters and one brother."

Gerda was born to **Peter and Stina Frykman** August 26, 1880 in Sweden.

ABOVE LEFT: Photo Courtesy of Evansville Historical Foundation; ABOVE RIGHT: Gerda with Luci and grandkids (Evansville Historical)

Frank Anderson

Frank Anderson was born in Princeton, Illinois in April 22, 1892. He was born to John P. Anderson and Ollie (Olivia Olofsdotter) both emigrated from Sweden. He had four brothers: Oscar, Victor, Hemming, and Alvin and two sisters **Minnie** and Selma (or Alma). Besides Wynat Bureau, Illinois, they lived in Medalia, Minnesota, and then to Erdahl Township in 1915. He volunteered for the draft for World War I, June 5, 1917. The three major battles of this company (Co D3 Pioneer Infantry) were Champagne Marne in 1918, one of the most decisive battles of the World War I, fought over a four-day period (July 15-18, 1918), Saint Mihiel, September 1918, and Meuse Argonne,1918. The last two battles were known as the bloodiest.

According to the *Grant County Herald*, March 8, 1962, "Frank Anderson, a former resident of Erdahl Township and a World War I veteran, passed away at Elbow Lake Friday. He had been in poor health a number of years and had his residence in Elbow Lake."

Minnie Evelyn Anderson

Minnie was born March 1886 in Illinois to John Anderson and Ollie (Olivia) Olofdotter. In 1900 they lived in Wyanet, Bureau, Illinois; In 1910 the family lived in Madelia, Mn. She is not listed with John and Olivia after 1910. However, in 1920 and in the 1930 census, a Minnie E. Anderson is a patient in the Fergus Falls State Hospital, Fergus Falls, Minnesota. Knowing she died in Fergus Falls, we believe this may be her. In the 1920 Census she is listed as widowed and in the 1930 Census she is listed as divorced (maybe divorced status was more acceptable by the 1930s). Also on a family tree on Ancestry.com , one researcher has her listed as married to an Alfred Sanlund in Illinois. In 1910 she is listed as single on the census. So all after 1910 is conjecture at this point.

The *Grant County Herald*, March 16, 1933, "Funeral services for Minnie Anderson were held March 7 at Zionsborg church...The deceased is survived by five brothers, Victor of Barrett; Oscar, Frank and Henning of Elbow Lake, and Alvin of Ashby.

Interment was at Zionsborg cemetery. The pall bearers were Oscar Malmgren, Victor Malmgren, J.P. Frykman, Ludwig Erickson, Frank Calson and Gilbert Anderson.

Ben Barlow's Sister

Since the church official records were burned, the caretaker's records had to be used. This one is a bit sketchy. All there is is a foot stone and the site is recorded as "Ben Barlow's sister." The burial was between 1880-1917.

Now Ben was the son of Ole T. Barlow who came from Norway and married Anna Mithome. According to the *Satterlie Saga* (a family history of the Saterlies), Ole and Anna lived in Ridgeway, Iowa and had five children—three boys and two girls. Anna died in 1887. Ole then moved to the Evansville area where his brother Joe lived. Here he met and married Sonneva Saterlie born March 8, 1842 Feios, Norway, June 24, 1888. They had one child who died in infancy.

Ben's other sisters grew to adulthood and moved away from this area and were still living when Ben died.

The 1895 census showed that Ole (54) and Sophie (an Americanization of Sonneva)(already 52) lived on the farm with no children except Sivert Satterlie, who was Sonneva's nephew, lived with them.

And 1905 and the 1910 census showed only Ole and Sophie. Based on this, we believe that Ben Barlow's sister is the infant of Ole and Sophie Barlow who are both buried in the Erdahl cemetery.

Capitola Barron

Capitola J. was born June 22, 1888, to **Charles and Christianna Peterson** (sister Beatrice and **Vivian** (Sowers), brothers Carl and Cecil and Clinton). She grew up on a farm in Lien township, Grant county, MN.

She was married Justin Hollis Albro, son of Norman and Hattie Albro, and lived in Minneapolis, according to the 1920 and 1930 census. He was a clerk for Joss and Ohlman in the 1918 directory. By 1937, he was a lawyer and Capitola was listed as a finisher at Model Launderers and Cleaners. After that, I lose him, but the 1948's voter registration shows him with his spouse Mrs. Annette Albro in Los Angeles, and in 1958, at 9142 Lampson, Garden Grove, CA. He died in 1963, in California. However, nothing more of Capitola was found on Ancestry.com.

I also cannot find divorce or remarriage to Barron or an obituary. Nonetheless, Capitola died September 2, 1972, in Hennepin County.

Carolina Bok

Carolina Bok was the daughter of Sven and Martha Bok and was born about June 1870 in Sweden. She immigrated to America when she was only 13 years old.

According to the passenger list she was with her mother Martha 45, (Carl) 15, and James 4, she arrived in New York on the ship *Lydian Monarch* on May 29, 1883. The handwriting is difficult to read but what was 'james' could be John, who is John Swenson. It was common for sons to take their father's first name and add 'son' in order to make a new surname. So John Bok becomes John Swenson, as we see in the later census.

This is not the same John Swenson buried at Zionsborg. Carolina is listed on the 1900 census as 29 living with Swen, Martha, and her brother John (24).

Borgen Home Page

Above: August Borgen Homplace in Elk Lake Township. Picture taken in Early 1900s. and aerial view early 1950s

The Borgen story actually begins with homesteader Thomas Borgen, father of Gust Borgen. (*History of Grant and Douglas Counties*) Thomas Borgen born 1828 in Hjorring, Denmark learned the blacksmith trade as a young man. Then he and his wife Johanna (Christianson) Borgen born 1827 emigrated from Hjorring, Denmark in 1866. They settled in Chicago and then in Milwaukee until 1870. They then moved to Evansville township Section 20 and homesteaded on 160 acres east of Davidson Lake. They had five children: Adolph, Kate (Alldrin), John, Gust, and Peter. Thomas was a private in the Spanish American War. He retired and moved to Evansville for 20 years before his death. "As a farmer and stockman, Thomas Borgen was successful and was recognized as one of the substantial men of the county, respected for his many sterling qualities of true manhood." He and his wife are buried in Oak Grove Cemetery at Evansville, Minnesota.

August Borgen was only 3 weeks old when his family immigrated. He owned a farm in Elk Lake Township sections 9 (where his home was) and 16 and built a home in Barrett for retirement. The old Abercrombie stage route cut right through his property in section 9.

August "Gust" and Julia and Ida Borgen

August Borgen was born in Hjorring, Denmark in 1866 to Thomas and Johanna Borgen. When he was only 3 weeks old he immigrated to America with his parents. In 1870, his parents settled in Evansville township.

In 1896 he married **Julia Anna** Peterson (Annie). Their first child, **a girl**, was born and died April 2, 1887. Then May 2, 1898 Edwin Thomas was born and **Helmer** Ingerman was born September 20, 1899. However, when **Joseph A.** was born July 9, 1901, Annie contracted tuberculosis and died a couple of weeks after his birth. Joseph died October 30, 1901. August chose to have his wife and two infants buried at Zionsborg Cemetery. Annie had grown up on a farm nearby and her parents Ed and Ingeborg Peterson still lived there.

In 1906 he was united in marriage to **Ida** Dorothy Strand. She had one son, Severin, born August 20, 1897, who was adopted by August.

He enjoyed whittling wood and it was always important to him to take care of the graves of his family buried at Zionsborg. August passed away January 1949. He had a large granite monument erected on the Borgen plot. Legend says that the monument was delivered from St. Cloud in 3 parts, using three teams of horses and wagons and then was assembled and sealed with lead into place on the cemetery plot. (information and pictures submitted by Joan Roe, granddaughter). Gust died January 11, 1949.

Julia "Annie" Borgen

Julia Anna (Annie) was born to Ed (Odd) and Igeborg Mebust Peterson in 1874. Both of Norwegian decent. According to the1880 Census, Julia lived with her parents in Salem township, Olmstead county along with three brothers: Ole, Peter and Sever.

She married **August** Borgen in Douglas County in 1896. Their first child, **a girl**, was born and died April 2, 1887. Then May 2, 1898 Edwin Thomas was born and Helmer Ingerman was born September 20, 1899. **Joseph A**. was born July 9th and died October 30, 1901. At the Age of 27, Annie contracted tuberculosis and died a couple of weeks after Joseph was born. August chose to have his wife and two infants buried at Zionsborg Cemetery. Annie had grown up on a farm nearby and her parents Ed and Ingeborg Peterson still lived there.(Pictures courtesy Joan Roe)

Ida D. Borgen

Ida was born in 1877 (parents unknown but there is an Ida (8) born to Peder and Mollie Strand living in Lien township, Grant County in 1885 with three sisters—Maria 10 and Bertha 4—and one brother Marcus.)

In 1900 when she was 22 she was a servant for CA Pederson taking care of his two children Arthur and Selma. She is widowed at this time and has a son Severin Arneson (2). In 1905, she is living with August Borgen. They were married in 1906 in Barrett.

L to R - Edwin, Severin & Helmer
Ida (Strand) & August Borgen

Ida died at the Barrett Hospital after a brief illness in 1917.

Joseph Borgen and Baby Borgen

August and Julia Anna (Peterson) Borgen's first child, a girl, was born and died April 2, 1987. **Joseph A. Borgen** was born July 9th and died October 30, 1901. His parents were August and Julia (Annie) Borgen.

Annie contracted tuberculosis and died a couple of weeks after Joseph was born at the age of 27.

Helmer I. and Pearl Borgen

Helmer Ingeman Borgen was born September 20, 1899 to **August and Julia (Peterson)Borgen** in Elk Lake township, Grant County, Minnesota. He was the third son.

November 12, 1929, when he was 30 he married **Pearl Myrtle Simonson** 21. They lived in Barrett with Gust. By this time, both Helmer's mother **Julia** and step-mother **Ida** were dead. Helmer worked for local merchants including Barett Oil Company and the Barrett Hardware Company. They had one daughter Joan Opal (Roe). Helmer was chief of the Barrett Fire Department and enjoyed square dancing. [information from Joan Roe, daughter and census] Helmer died July 7, 1985.

Pearl Myrtle Borgen

Pearl was born in Dawson, Minnesota, May 13, 1906, to Simon Simonson and Oline Vollan Simonson, both of Norwegian descent. She had six sisters—Alma, Alvine, Mathilde, Olga, and Edna—and one brother,

Selfred. In 1910, The family was living in Blooming Valley, Grant County, South Dakota. The census also showed Pearl (4) was "living" with her maternal grandfather Peder H. Vollan and his family in Cerro Gordo Township, Lac Qui Parle. According to the 1920 Census, the Simonson family were all living in Cerro Gordo Township, Lac Qui Parle County.

November 12, 1929, Pearl and **Helmer Borgen** were married. They made their home in Barrett with Gust, Helmer's father. While Helmer worked for local merchants including Barett Oil Company and the Barrett Hardware Company, Pearl was a housewife and mother. They had one daughter **Joan Opal (Roe)**.

Pearl enjoyed square dancing and crocheting. Her good caramel rolls, brownies and chocolate chip cookies are some of the warm memories shared by her daughter. [Information and pictures from Joan Roe, daughter and census]

Clow Home Page

2012 picture of the Emery Clow home; and the second house is the house that Merritt and Helen lived in and raised Sharon and Doug during the time they attended Zionsborg Church. See Frank A. and John O Peterson for the land map.

According to Sharon Kalland, his daughter, Merrit's father' (Emery) farm was just north of Barrett. (See map) His maternal grandfather was George Washinton Lovell, and had served in the Civil War. During the Colonial era the Lovell family came from England and settled in Virginia and eventually moving west.

The Clow family, perhaps spelled Clough or MacClough, originally came from Scotland. The Clows were in America in the 1700s and moved

26

to Canada at the time of the Revolutionary War of 1776. Later they moved back and settled in Illinois, Kansas, Wisconsin, and Truman, MN.

One family story told by Merritt was that when the James brothers were robbing banks around the country, one day they rode into the Clow farm near Truman and asked to water their horses.

Merritt and Helen rented the Frank A. Peterson farm in Elk Lake township section 2 and 3.

Merritt and Helen Clow

Merritt Clow

"**Merritt Raymond Clow** was born Sept. 5, 1904, in Truman, MN, to Emery and Etta (Lovell) Clow, the third of seven siblings. While still a child he moved with his family to Grant County. As a young man he went with friend to Montana and spent several years working on ranches and helping with the farm harvests. He returned to Minnesota in the early 1930s, married Helen Marion Swenson on July 3, 1936, and began farming near Evansville and Barrett in Douglas and Grant Counties. Merritt and Helen had two children, Sharon Adele (1938) and Douglas Merritt (1942).

Merritt retired from farming in the late-1960s and he and Helen moved to Alexandria, MN. He continued to work on local farms and for Green Thumb until he retired in his late 80s. Due to poor physical health, Merritt moved to Bethany Home in 1996, where he was known and loved for his friendliness, jokes and general good nature. He passed away early June 18, 2000, after having visited one last time with Helen, his children and son-in-law and two youngest grandchildren..." (from his Douglas County Historical obituary.)

Helen Clow

Helen was born October 22, 1906, to **John and Mathilda Swenson**. She was the eldest of 5 children, Helen, Alice, Alden, **Jennie**, and **Gladys**.

"She attended District 49 grade school and graduated from Evansville High School. After graduation Helen worked as a waitress at Osterberg's Café in Alexandria and Blakes by the lakes. Later she moved to St.Paul and worked at the St. Paul Hotel. She married Merritt Clow July 3, 1936. Together they farmed near Evansville and later Barrett and raised two children, Sharon and Douglas.

"After retiring from farming Helen and Merritt moved to Alexandria. For many years they lived next door to their daughter and her family, sharing the joys of everyday life together...

Helen honored God with a living faith. She taught Sunday school, served as superintendent and helped in other church activities for many years at Zionsborg Lutheran Church. In her later years she regularly worshiped at First Lutheran in Alexandria. Helen had many interests. She enjoyed farm life, the outdoors, fishing and hunting. She especially loved her flower garden. In her early sixties, she started oil and watercolor painting. She also enjoyed needle work and especially looked forward to 'Hobby Night' with her daughter, sisters, and nieces. Helen loved entertaining and seeing that everyone was well fed. During her retirement, Helen was an Avon representative until the age of 91. She was a resident of Knute Nelson Memorial Home from September 1999 until her death July, 2000" (*Echo Press* obituary 7/26/2000).) Pictures from Evansville Historical and Sharon Kalland

Sigrid Dahlen

According to the *Evansville Enterprise* May 25, 1939, **Sigrid** was born March 17, 1903, in Delaware township, Grant County, MN to **Mr. and Mrs. P.H. Nelson**. She had 2 brothers—Adolph and Ernest; and four sisters---Mrs. Arthur Johnson, Mrs. Hjalmer Johnson, Miss Hilda Nelson, and Mrs. Esther Ostlund. "She grew to womanhood in the Barrett community, and through confirmation, became a member of the Zionsborg Lutheran Church, of which her parents were also members. On May 29, 1929 she was united in marriage to Mr. Leonard C. Dahlen. Their home was blessed with three children, Betty Jane, **Donald** and Darlene. They resided on a farm near the Zionsborg Church."

... "Her health had been failing for some time and this, augmented by an attack of influenza caused her death..." She died May 18, 1939.

Home place as it looked in 2012. See Solberg home place.

Donald Dahlen

According to his obituary (DCHS), **Donald** was born November 24, 1930, at Barrett, MN to Leonard C. and **Sigrid** I. (Nelson) Dahlen. He was baptized and confirmed into the Lutheran faith and attended school in Barrett and later in Evansville where he graduated. He farmed with his father until 1954 when he was inducted into the United States Army until 1956.

He married Beverly Thompson of Herman, MN. They made their home in Anoka where he died June 30, 1991. He had been employed at the Northwest Ordinance Plant of Minneapolis for several years. He was retired at the time of his death. Memorial Services were held July 13, 1991 at Erdahl Lutheran Church in Erdahl. His ashes were interred in Zionsborg.

He had four sons David, Douglas (Pam), Duane (Cindy), and Darren; and three daughters— Deanne (Mrs. Todd Jorgenson), Darla and Donia all of Coon Rapids. His sisters are Betty (Mrs. Andrew Westman) Garfield and Darlene (Mrs. Eugene Olson, Crystal Lake, Illinois. His step-mother was Lucille Dahlen and step-siblings Warren and Sandy. (Evansville Historical Foundation)

Alice Kathryn Peterson-Domas

Alice Kathryn "Katy" was the only child of **Alfred and Olive (Huseth) Peterson**; she was born December 17, 1925, in Barrett. She married Robert G. Domas, June 24, 1988, and worked in Social Services.

She died in Minneapolis, MN, March 18, 2007. No obituary was found in Grant County or in the Minneapolis, St. Paul obituary archive.

Per Erickson Home Page

Per (Peter) Erickson was born August 14, 1830 in Varmland, Sweden to Erick Johnson and Marit (Nelsdotter). He married **Marit (Mary)** Persdotter or Larsdotter daughter of Per Larson in 1850. He immigrated to America in 1866. He bought land in Urness township Section 6, just east of Nils Aldrin's homestead. The farm was located next to Per's sister's homestead **(Olof and Maria Alldrin)**.

"Their first home was nothing more than a dugout with whitewashed wall. Later Chippewa Indians and neighbors helped them build a small two story house." Peter was one of charter members and one of the first officers of Zionsborg. He along with **Erik Malmgren** and **Ole Alberts** were the first trustees. (Information from his great-granddaughter Gladys Gerhardt)

Peter and Mary Erickson

Per (Peter) Erickson was born August 14, 1830 in Varmland, Sweden to Erick Johnson and Marit (Nelsdotter). He married **Marit (Mary)** Persdotter or Larsdotter daughter of Per Larson in 1850. According to his great-granddaughter, Peter immigrated and arrived July 6, 1866 aboard the ship Mauritius and worked at the Pillsbury Flour Mills. He established a homestead in Urness township. And Mary came in 1868 in a "sailboat" along with their four children. The boat's provisions were mostly herring, bread and occasionally potatoes. The passengers were transferred to another boat for the last days of eleven weeks and four days. They came to Minneapolis and then to St. Cloud by rail, and then by wagon to their homestead in Urness township.

Their first home was a dugout with white washed sod walls. At one time, Peter had to work in Minneapolis at the Pillsbury Flour Mills to help support his family. He and his wife had 10 children—Mary (Bristol) 1859, **Ole Per, Maria** "Maggie" 1863, Christine 1865, **Albin** 1869, **Edward** 1871, **Ida** Helmina 1873, Selma 1875, **Peter Hjalmer** 1878, and George 1881.

Peter was one of charter members and one of the first officers of Zionsborg. He along with **Erik Malmgren** and **Ole Alberts** were the first trustees. He died October 24, 1896, as a result of being crushed in a wagon accident in rural Evansville. (Information from Gladys Gerhardt, great- granddaughter) The headstone reads, "The Lord gave. The Lord took. Exalted is the name of the Lord."

Marit Erickson

Marit Erickson was born September 23, 1835, on a farm near Torsby Varmland, Sweden to Per and Gertrude Larson. She married Per (Peter) Erickson son of John Johnson and Marit (Nelsdotter) in 1850. She and her husband raised 10 children on their homestead in Urness township.

Mary, Ole Per, Maria, and Christine immigrated with their mother and father; the rest were born in America. According to his great-granddaughter, Mary came in 1868 in a "sailboat" along with their four children. The boat's provisions were mostly herring, bread and occasionally potatoes. The passengers were transferred to another boat for the last days of the journey of eleven weeks and four days. They came to Minneapolis and then to St. Cloud by rail. Then by wagon to their homestead in Urness township. Their first home was a dugout with white washed sod walls. At one time, Peter had to work in Minneapolis at the Pillsbury Flour Mills to help support his family . Marit died July 7, 1920, perhaps from the complications due to a fractured hip.

She was a charter member of the Zionsborg Church. . (Information from Gladys Gerhardt, great- granddaughter)

Her children were Mary (Bristol) 1859, Ole Per, Maria "**Maggie**" 1863, Christine 1865, **Albin** 1869, **Edward** 1871, **Ida** Helmina 1873, Selma 1875, **Peter Hjalmer** 1878, and **George** 1881.

Maria (Maggie) Albin, Peter Hjalmer, and Edward Erickson

Maggie was born August 4, 1863, in Varmland, Sweden **to Per and Marit Erickson**. She immigrated to America with her mother and siblings in 1868.

She married Olaf Lyden, an engineer, in 1892. They made their home in Minneapolis. In 1893 she had a son Arthur; however, she died a year later at the age of 31 of tuberculosis. Olaf remarried to Kristina Strand and they had three children. Picture from Evansville Historic Foundation

Albin, Per Hjalmer, and Edward

Albin was born to **Per (Peter) and Mary Erickson** June 12, 1869 and died May 11, 1898 at the age of 28. **Per Hjalmer** was born to **Per (Peter) and Mary Erickson** September 7, 1878. He died February 9, 1899, at the age of 20. **Edward** was born January 24, 1871, **to Per and Marit Erick-**

son. He died August 19, 1902, at the age of 33.

"It has been said they (Maggie, Albin, Per Hjalmer and Edward) died from consumption or tuberculosis...The family left the farm heartbroken after so many deaths. With George very young when the last adult man died, there wasn't much to do but give up. Marit moved into Evansville after she and Ida engineered an auction." (family history provided by Gladys Gerhardt)

George Erickson

Born April 13, 1881 to **Per (Peter) and Marit (Mary) Erickson, George** was one of eleven children. He died September 6, 1958.

"George Erickson never married. At the age of 19 he started work as a store clerk in Elbow Lake. In Minneapolis he worked in the Grain Exchange where grain stocks were traded. It was founded in 1881. He lived a few blocks from his brother Joe in Minneapolis. He was a distinguished looking man and dressed well. He died when he was robbed and beaten, probably because someone thought he had money" (Bonee Erickson story and picture) (Note: I have Joe as his nephew)

Ida Erickson

Born January 29, 1873, **to Per (Peter) and Marit Erickson,** Ida Helmina was one of ten children. According to Bonee Erickson, "Ida never married. She lived in Minneapolis most of her life but stayed with her sisters Selma in California and Mary in Evansville. In the early years, Ida worked as domestic help but developed excellent seamstress skills. In the 1950's, she lived and worked for Amluxen family who owned a fabric company."Ida died July 23, 1950. Pictures from Evansville Historical Foundation

Ole Per and Martha Erickson

Ole Per was born in Torsby, Varmland, Sweden to **Per (Peter) and Mary Erickson** July 26, 1861. He came to America with his parents and three other siblings in 1868 when he was only 6. As the story goes, he would climb the rigging and slide down while aboard ship wearing out his trousers.

He and his family settled in Urness township on a farm. He married **Martha Kaja Borg** June 4, 1887; and they set up a home in Erdahl township. They had 10 children—**Levi, Mabel**, Leonard, **Ludwig**, Edwin, William, Joseph, Waldemer, Lloyd, and Vennette. He died February 23, 1911. (information and pictures submitted by Gladys Gerhardt, granddaughter)

House in 1940'es

Martha Kajsa Erickson

Martha Kajsa Borg was born January 6, 1862, in Varmland, Sweden to John P. Borg and Kajsa Andersdotter. She immigrated with her father 1883 to establish a homestead near Melby. (see Carrie Lindstrom)

She married **Ole P. Erickson** June 4, 1887;and they set up a home in Erdahl township. They had 10 children—**Levi**, **Mabel**, Leonard, **Ludwig**, Edwin, **William**, Joseph, Waldemare, Lloyd, and Vennette. She died July 3, 1918 from pernicious anemia. (information and pictures submitted by Gladys Gerhardt, granddaughter)

Back: Ludwig, Leonard, Mabel, and Levi. Front: Joseph (on lap) Ole, William, baby Waldemare, Edwin. Not born Lloyd and Venette

Levi Erickson

Levi Ferdinand Erickson was born July 15, 1888, in Erdahl township, Minnesota, **to Ole Per and Martha Kajsa (Borg) Erickson.** Levi was one of ten children— Levi, **Mabel**, Leonard, Ludwig, Edwin, **William**, Joseph, Otto, Lloyd, and Edna.

The 1910 census shows a Levi Erickson, farm hand age 21. In 1917, he registered for the draft at the age of 29 and was listed as single. He married Ethel Imogene Ackerson (a neighbor girl). In 1920 the census shows Levi and Ethel living in Seattle, Washington, with their 4 month old daughter Myrtle, who was born in Washington; and his occupation was boiler maker, and according to Bonee Erickson he was working at the shipyards. (They were living with Russel and Selma Dymond , Ole's sister). The 1930 shows them living back in Erdahl township, Minnesota, with 10 year old Myrtle and Marjorie who was almost 5. 1940 Census shows Levi (51), Ethel (50) and Marjorie (14) living here yet.

They spent their winters in Washington with one of their daughters after retiring. He died September 2, 1969. His wife Ethel died December 21, 1976, in Olympia, Washington, where she is buried.

ABOVE: Picture of Ethel and Levi from the 1964 Zionsborg's congregation picture. (The two ladies behind them are L to R Anna Elvrum and Hilma Frykman).

RIGHT: Levi as a young man (picture from Bonee Erickson)

Mabel Victoria Erickson

Born November 6, 1889, to Ole P. and Kjasa (Borg) Erickson, **Mabel** was one of ten children. She died September 5, 1975 in Barrett, Minnesota. Mabel V. Erickson picture courtesty of Bonee Erickson.

William Dewey Erickson

William Erickson was born September 19, 1898, **to Ole and Martha Erickson**. He was one of nine children—**Levi, Mabel**, Leonard, **Ludwig**, Edwin, **William**, Joseph, Lloyd and Vinette. As his obituary says, he was "associated with Westinghouse Corp. in Newark as an engineer.

William is on the right

He had never married" and at the time of his death November 29, 1958, Mabel Erickson was living in Chicago and Vinnette (Noby) in Willmar, MN. Levi was in Barrett, Leonard and Joseph in Minneapolis, Ludvig in Erdahl and Lloyd in Brooklyn. Pictures courtesy Evansville Historical Foundation.

Ludwig McCornel and Alma Erickson

Ludwig Erickson was born January 23, 1893, in Erdahl township, Minnesota, **to Ole Per and Martha Kajsa (Borg) Erickson**. Ludwig was one of ten children—**Levi, Mabel**, Leonard, Edwin, **William**, Joseph, Otto, Lloyd, and Edna.

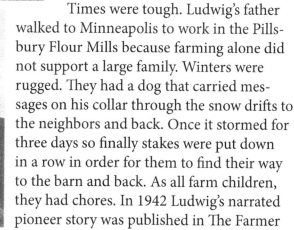

Times were tough. Ludwig's father walked to Minneapolis to work in the Pillsbury Flour Mills because farming alone did not support a large family. Winters were rugged. They had a dog that carried messages on his collar through the snow drifts to the neighbors and back. Once it stormed for three days so finally stakes were put down in a row in order for them to find their way to the barn and back. As all farm children, they had chores. In 1942 Ludwig's narrated pioneer story was published in The Farmer Magazine detailing his grandparents' journey to America and settling in Erdahl township.

Ludwig eventually secured railroad land granted by the government. He married **Alma V. Johnson** March 29, 1919, in Barrett. They had two children—Gladys (Rohloff-Gerhardt) and **Kenneth**. Ludwig was an inventor of the Staplematic and the Erickson Proofer. He had a wind-mill for charging batteries for his radio in the '30s. He was also noted for being thrifty. He along with other family moved to the Hackensack area. There he was so poor he could not even buy overshoes. According to Gladys, times were so bad that he moved back to Erdahl township and was never that poor again. Ludwig and Alma lived on a farmstead on County Road 10, four miles west of Zionsborg and then moved to a farmstead on County Road 5, two miles west and 1/4 mile north of Zi-onsborg. (information and pictures from Gladys Gerhardt)

Alma Victoria (Johnson) Erickson

Alma was born in a dugout on the **John Johnson** homestead in Erdahl township three and a half miles NE of Barrett, MN. She was the second child of John and Lena, on February 25, 1889. She died November 30, 1963 at the age of 74. As a child she played with her sisters Selma and Clara.

She married **Ludwig Erickson** March 29, 1919, in Barrett. They had two children Gladys M. (Rohloff-Gerhardt) and **Kenneth Lloyd Erick-son**. She enjoyed playing the guitar and gardening. Her daughter Gladys remembers that Alma was quite particular about too much makeup, especially lipstick and did not approve of smoking. She was especially anxious to have her children be good Christians, to live right, and keep good company. She was known for her sincerity and kindness. She enjoyed company and giving them treats of coffee and homemade bread with butter and jam, molasses cookies, or doughnuts. At one time, they along with other family moved to the Hackensack area. However, life

Alma Victoria Johnson + Ludwig [Elgu?]
the Cornai Erickson m March 31, 1919 [?]

there times was so bad that the moved back to Erdahl township.

Ludwig and Alma lived on a farmstead on County Road 10, 4 miles west of Zionsborg and then moved to a farmstead on County Road 5, 2miles west and 1/4 mile north of Zionsborg. (information submitted by Gladys Gerhardt, daughter)

Kenneth Lloyd and Ethel Erickson

Kenneth was the second child of **Ludwig and Alma Erickson**. He was born November 24, 1923, in Hackensack, MN. (See Ludwig and Alma) His family moved back to Erdahl township as making a living in Northern Minnesota was very hard. He and his sister **Gladys (Rohloff-Gerhardt)** were the only children of Ludwig and Alma. He was in the medical division in the navy during World War II. While in Seattle at the Naval base, he was an ambulance driver on call. He was shipped out and served on a hospital ship in the South Pacific. His wife, **Ethel (Jones)**, was born Oct. 15, 1923. They were married Nov. 19, 1946. Kenneth worked at Alex Light & Power. Ethel was head bookkeeper at 3M in Alexandria before she retired. Kenneth died April 23, 1999, in Alexandria; and Ethel died July 15, 2009 in Alex. They had four children: Sharon (married James Hurley) lives in Moorhead. Gary (married Beata Faehnrich) lives in Willmar, Twins Roberta (married Gregory Habel – deceased 2010) and lives in Moorhead, Mn; and Rebecca (married Gary San Souci) lives in Willmar.

Kenneth was a very good singer; he and his sister sang together at many functions, including church programs, Luther League, 4-H, weddings, etc. He also sang on the radio in Fergus Falls. When he was very little he would sing for people, but had to sit under the table in order to do so. He was also a saxophone player in the Evansville High School band and a part of the men's chorus or octet that went to the State Competition.

According to his daughter Sharon Hurley, he "was a gentle, quiet man who loved his family...He was extremely hard working and completed the smallest task with perfection and pride. This could be seen in all areas of his life. The garbage men loved him because he would almost gift wrap the garbage.

Dad was a wonderful father. I remember an incident nearly 40 years ago when dad consoled me after classmates had said some hurtful things to me. I cried so hard, but Dad came and talked to me and made me feel better.

Dad worked very hard to see that his family was provided for. Most of his life he worked two jobs. He saw that all of his children were able to go to college. He often said that he wished that he had gone to college, but he never stopped learning...

Dad was a person you called upon if you needed anything. He had just about everything stored in his garage and 3 sheds. He had no problem finding something because he had every item inventoried and written down. He was also the person you called if you needed something fixed...

Music was such an important area of dad's life. He loved to sing and dance. He was especially proud of getting together with his high school singing group at the last all-school reunion. At family gatherings with the cousins, he could always get Vonny to sing a song with him. Dad was quite the dancer. He loved to go to dances and he was so proud of winning the dance contest with mom.

Dad loved his gardens and being outside tinkering. Many men go fishing as a form of relaxation, but dad would go outside to pull a couple of weeds and tend to his garden for his form of relaxation. He was extremely proud of his vegetables and being able to share them.

I will miss you Dad, but I have fond memories of my life with you and the wonderful father that you have been." (submitted by his daughter-Sharon Hurley)

Kenneth Lloyd Erickson in Seattle 1945 21st Birthday

Ethel Erickson

Ethel Jane (Jones) Erickson was born on October 15, 1923 in Alexandria, MN: the youngest daughter of David and Matilda (Olsen) Jones. Her older sister is Inez (Leonard) Okerlund. Ethel went through the Alexandria Public Schools and graduated from Central High School in Alexandria in 1941. After graduation she moved to Chicago with a friend where she worked as a bookkeeper for a couple of years. When she returned to Alexandria, she met Kenneth Erickson.

On November 19, 1946, Ethel was united in marriage to **Kenneth L. Erickson** of Erdahl Township. Together they raised four children (see Kenneth's page). They also had seven wonderful grandchildren: Mitchell (Mindy) SansSouci of Oakdale, MN; Ryan Hurley (fiancée Kami Kosenko) of Raleigh, NC; Melissa (Clark) Hagen of Fargo, ND; Angela (Brady) Callaghan of Fargo, ND; Lisa (Tyson) Fairbanks of Alvord, TX; Allen Erickson of St. Cloud, MN; Bryan (Jeni) Erickson of St. Cloud, MN; great grandchildren Kylee and Eliana of St. Cloud, MN; Isabella and Sofia Fairbanks of Alvord, TX.

Ethel and Kenneth lived most of their married life in Alexandria, but the family also lived in Hastings, NE and Willmar, MN. Ethel's favorite job was working at the 3M Company where she worked for 15 years. Kenny and Ethel loved to take short trips throughout the state and to visit their children and grandchildren. They also had two wonderful gardens in the back yard where they grew many vegetables and flowers. That backyard was the center of many family gathering.

Daughter Sharon wrote of her mother, "She was like her birthstone: the opal... not colorful or splashy like diamonds, rubies, or emeralds but a rare gem with a hint of mystery. When you look at the opal, you first see a basic solid white stone. Then you notice subtle hints of different color. That was mother. She was the strong center of our family. She was always there if you were sad, happy, needed advice, or just an ear to listen. Mother was a private person. She kept many of her thoughts to herself, but she would subtly let you know how she felt about something if she thought it necessary. She was also extremely generous and thoughtful. She managed to send special occasion cards so that they would arrive on that special day. During the last eight years she never let that wheelchair get her down. She managed to live independently at Windmill Ponds in her own apartment. She also had a wonderful circle of friends and enjoyed each day. She was a great lady." (information and pictures from Sharon Hurley, daughter)

Oliver Fedje and Emma Fedje

Oliver Fedje was born July 27, 1881 to Andrew and Margaret (Johnson) Fedje. He was one of 9 children Emma, Oliver, Charley, Lewis, Elmer, Benjamin, Clara, Oscar, and Clarence. They lived in Urness Township of Douglas County. He was confirmed by Rev. Sattre in St. Petri Church of Douglas County. According to the *Grant County Herald* October, 8, 1959, "Mr. Fedje grew to manhood on his father's farm and homesteaded at Grenora, N.D.

He married **Emma Caroline Setterlund** April 26, 1931. They set up their home in Elk Lake Township farming his father's farm for only two years when his health failed and he moved to Barrett and then to his brother-in-law **Victor's** home. He had six brothers—Louie, Oscar, Clarence, Charley, Benjamin, and Elmer; and two sisters-- Emma Kadrie and Clara Fommering both of Minneapolis." He died April 4, 1959.

Emma Fedje

Emma was born 20 March 1886 in Erdahl Twp., Grant Co., MN, to **Peter and Karin** (Johnsdotter) **Setterlund**. Her siblings included Anna, Mary, Nils, Karl, Andrew, Oscar, Johan, Ole, Anders, and **Axel Victor**. Emma played the church organ at Zionsborg for many years. Even with extreme arthritis in her hands, she is remembered for her "exuberant" organ playing and having a voice that needed no microphone. She was also known to walk the six miles to church. According to the Zionsborg History notes, "She will be remembered for her striking personality, her sociable kindness, her great interest in people, her work as Erdahl Elk Lake correspondent to the *Grant County Herald* as well as her musical ability... When the church closed its doors in November of 1965, Emma became the recipient of the old pump organ..." She died September 18, 1973.

1942

Best Christmas Wishes

LEFT: Photo courtesy of Evansville Historical Foundation

RIGHT: Emma and her sister

Ernest Forsberg

Ernest Gustaf Forsberg was born September 7, 1881, to Carl and Ida Forsberg. He died March 11, 1887. Little is known about this family. After his death , it appears that they may have moved to Souris, Bottineau, North Dakota, as many families did from this area. If so, this C.G. and Ida Forsberg went on to have nine more children including another Ernest Forsberg. Ernest's father and brother are listed as builders of the Swedish Zion Stone Church in Bottineau County, ND. Other builders included family members who left this area including Eklunds, Backmans, John Schroeder, and others. (from *Stone Church, a Prairie Parable* by Gene Wunderlich.

One of their children, Amelia married Nils John Frykman , son of **Jon Nilsson Frykman** and a Mrs. John Frykman who died before he married Maria Johnson (according to two family trees found on Ancestry.com)

Ernest Franzen

Ernest was born of Swedish descent in September 22, 1886, to Peter and Mary (Johnson) Franzen of Rockford, MN. It is unclear where exactly he was born but it is listed as Minnesota. He had three sisters---Elvina, Ella, and Ida. Ernest was living with John and Helena Peterson as a farm laborer according to the 1910 Census. He married **Hilda Jenstad** August 30, 1911, in Minneapolis.

In 1920 they rented a farm near Buffalo, MN. Then returned to the Jenstad farm, where they lived with her sister. He died March 7, 1956, in an accident involving a train. According to an article in the March 8, 1956, *Park Region Echo*, his car stalled on the railroad track in Barrett, MN. He had two women passengers, Mrs. Andrew Betland and Mrs. Art Johnson, who had gotten out of the car. It was thought that he was pushing the car across the tracks when he was hit. Local families remember Ernest repairing shoes and work boots for them.

Hilda Franzen

Hilda Franzen was born November 19, 1891 to **Ole and Mary Jenstad** of Elk Lake Township. According to the *Evansville Enterprise* October 10, 1929, "She was confirmed in Lincoln Norwegian Lutheran Church. She was married to Mr. E.H. Franzen in 1911, who now survives her. Death was due to an illness of about a year, during time specialists were sought and everything done to relieve her but on Tuesday morning, Oct. 1, she passed away at the age of 37 yrs., 10 mo., and 20 days. Besides her husband she is survived by one sister **Mary** and her brother Garder [sic.]"(should be Gunder).

Ingeborg Frykman

(From Grandell Unger Family Tree ancestry. com) **Ingeborg** Persdotter- Nilsson was born April 5, 1817 in Varmland, Sweden. Parents were possibly Per Olsson and Brita Jonsdotter according to a number of family trees on ancestry.com. She married Nils Nilsson June 24, 1841. He was a cabinet maker, coffin maker, and farmer. They had six children: **Nils Nilsson Frykman, Per Nilsson Frykman, Jon Nilsson Frykman,** John Nilsson Bachman, **Gertrude** Nilsdotter Frykman and Lisa Nilsdotter. Ingeborg died in 1889. Here is here Swedish emigration record.

Ingeborg
Birth Year: abt 1817
Gender: Kvinna (Female)
Place of Origin: Fryksände Värmland Län, Sverige
Destination: New York
Record Date: 18 maj 1883 (18 May 1883)
Port of Departure: Göteborg
Database Name: EmiHamn
Archive Call Number: 22:611:31402
Traveling Companion: M
Principal Person: Nilson Joh

Gertrude (Hjertrue) Frykman

Gertrude was born July 9, 1850 in Varmland, Sweden to **Nils and Ingeborg (Persdotter) Nilsson**. According to David Frykman, **Ingeborg** and

44

Gertrude were brought to America by their sons after Ingeborg's husband Nils died. The Frykman Family History states, "Gertrude was un-married and worked in various homes. She worked for **Gust Westling** as a house-keeper. **Bertil** and **Alvin** remember her coming to church at Zionsborg." (Frykman Family History)

Gertrude died March 2, 1931, from heart failure and senility in the Bethany Home in Alexandria. I found a Gertrude Nilsson 35 and Nils Johan Nilsson 8(born 1878) Fryksande, Varmland

Sweden, arriving in America destination Evansville... arriving July 5, 1886, on the ship Louisa. This matches but no Ingeborg. **See Ernest Forsberg** for more information on Nils Johan Nilsson. Picture courtesy Evansville Historical Foundation.

Nils Nilson Frykman Home Page

Nils Nilson Frykman was born Feb 23, 1842 to Nils and Igeborg (Persdotter)Nilson in Varmland Sweden. He married Brita Katrina (**Christine-Stina**) Jonasdotter September 10, 1871 in Fryksande, Varmland, Sweden. His occupation in Sweden was a forest ranger. They immigrated and arrived in Alexandria July 9, 1881. According to his great-grandson Allen Frykman, in 1882 the Railroad was selling land; Nils liked the prairie land near Barrett and purchased 160 acres for $25. That building site is now own by his great grandson Dwayne Frykman. The original homestead has remained in the Frykman family ever since Nils and Stina first settled here. They homestead in Erdahl township section 35 on 186.39 acres.

Nils Nilson Frykman

Nils Nilson Frykman was born February 29, 1842 to Nils and **Ingeborg** (Persdotter)Nilson in Svenneby, Varmland Sweden. He married Brita Katrina (**Christina**) Jonasdotter September 10, 1871 in Fryksande Lutheran Church, Fryksande, Sweden.

"His occupation in Sweden was a forest ranger. Nils stood six feet tall and had black hair. They immigrated and arrived in Alexandria July 9, 1881. He became a US citizen May 24, 1897. Nils and Christina changed their last name to Frykman when they became US citizens. "Nils could see no great future in Sweden and was not satisfied working as a forest ranger. He also believed the move to America would benefit his family. In 1881 they took a train to Oslo, Norway, to catch the boat to America. In Oslo no one at the ticket office had heard of Alexandria, MN. The ticket seller was prepared to sell him a ticket to Alexandria, Egypt! (Thank goodness they got that straightened out.)

He and Christine had 9 children: **Nels John, Peter**, August, Anna, Christine "Kristine" born in Sweden- Victor, Maria "Minnie," Emily, and Alma born in the U.S. In 1882 the railroad was selling land; Nils liked the prarie land near Barrett and purchased 160 acres for $25. That building site is now owned by his great-grandson Dwayne Frykman.

Nils whittled and made toys of wood for his children and furniture for the house. Two of these pieces are still being used by his great-grandson Alvin Frykman in their home in Elbow Lake, MN. Nils helped build

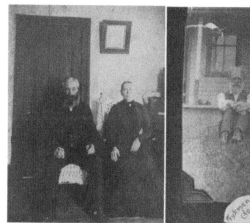

the first Zionsborg Church and was a charter member and officer of the church for 13 years.

He died Oct 9, 1922." (Al Frykman and Frykman Family History)

— NILS · CHRISTINA —
ALMA, VICTOR, MINNIE, AUGUST, EMILY, PETER, CHRISTINE, JOHN, A
50.TH WEDDING ANNIVERSARY 1871-1921
AT THE HOME OF SON, PETER FRYKMAN, EVANSVILLE, MIN

Stina Frykman

"Christine was born in 1843 to Jonas and Kirste (Larsdotter) Peterson. Her older sister (also Stina) married Per Frykman. Christina was very attractive with blue eyes and light brown hair. Christina made clothing for the family. She carded, spun, washed, dyed, and knitted wool garments and taught these skills to her children. Twine was braided and worn as belts. The woment took care of the cows; milking was considered women's work. The children had fun on the nearby lake in the summer and winter. She walked to the neighbors in bare feet (to save wear on her shoes) and then put them on when she arrived."(Frykman Family History) She died in 1929.

In the words of their daughter Emily, the "light" of Nils and Christina shines in the hearts of their children and will become a "star" for us to

47

follow. In the American tradition, it is not the "roots" that count so much as the "branches" and "leaves." (Al Frykman and Frykman Family History)

Jon Nels and Maria Frykman

Jon Nilsson Frykman was born Aug 26, 1847 in Varmland, Sweden to Nils Nilsson and Ingeborg Persdotter. He died June 7, 1923. He married **Maria** Johnson. See above. (picture courtesy of Evansville Historical Foundation)

Maria Frykman

According to the obituary in the *Grant County Herald*, she "was born in Varmland Sweden, April 1, 1860. (Johnson or Jonsdotter). She was baptized and confirmed in the Lutheran faith in her homeland. She came to America June 13, 1887 and was employed in St. Paul for four years after coming to this country.

On December 29, 1891, she was united in marriage to **Jon N. Frykman** at the Christine Lake parsonage by the late Rev. S. J. Kronberg and they established their home on the farm in Erdahl Township which the groom had purchased..."

She and John N. had six children: Victor Frykman, Clara (Mrs. Floyd Harrison), **Hilma, Oscar**, Anna (Mrs. Jule Elvrum), and a daughter (name unknown who preceded her in death) and one stepchild John Nels Frykman. She had one sister and two brothers who stayed in Sweden Karlina, August, and Otto Johnson.

"Mrs. Frykman was a member of the Zionsborg congregation and was active in the work of the ladies' aid and Women's Missionary societies. She possessed a pleasant disposition and was loved by all who knew her. Grandma Frykman, as she was affectionately called, welcomed everyone into the hospitality of her home. (picture courtesty Evansville Historical Foundation)

Hilma C. Frykman

Hilma Frykman was the daughter of **John Nils and Maria Frykman**. She was born February 23, 1894. In 1930, she is listed as a servant for the Herbert and Minnie Wagner, rural Pelican Rapids area. According to the 1940 Census, she worked as a housekeeper for the John Nygren family, who lived in Elbow Lake. She died June 23, 1960, from a heart attack. (picture from a Zionsborg Congregation picture)

Oscar Frykman

Oscar Julius Frykman was born to **John Nils and Maria Frykman** June 8, 1896. . According to the 1940 census, he had his sister Anna 43 and mother Maria 79 living with him. Oscar lived on the farm which is now part of Doug Frykman's pasture. He died December 6, 1968. (picture from a Zionsborg Congregation picture)

Nels J. and Clara Frykman

"**Nels Johan Frykman**, the son of **Nels and Christina Frykman**, was born August. 6, 1871, near Thorsby Wermland [sic], Sweden, and passed away at his home Sept. 10 at the age of 80 years, one month and four days.

He came to America with his parents, two brother and two sisters in 1881 and the family first settled at Holmes City. In the spring of 1882 they came to Erdahl township where they have resided since. He was confirmed in the Zionsborg church and has been a member of the congregation since.

On March 31, 1915, he was united in marriage to **Clara Wilhelmina**

Johnson, a distant cousin. To this union two children, Mrs. Haaken (Alice) Skarphol of Souris, N.D. and **Alvin**, living on the home farm were born.

Possessor of a beautiful bass voice, he had been a member of the church choir for over 30 years, In his younger days he had served as a church board and was honorary deacon at the time of his death..." (1951 obituary)

The Frykman Family History states that "...He was tall, slender, had blue eyes and brown hair. He lived on the "home farm" in Barrett all his life and went to the Barrett county school. ...He learned to play organ and was the church organist for many years... John owned the first steam-engine in the area and did threshing for the neighbors. John was rather quiet, kind and generous, and devoted to his family. He drove his father's 1911 Overland car, because his father Nils did not care to drive." He died September 7, 1951. Pictures from Frykman Family Tree and Alvin Frykman Family

John Nels driving, with his mother Christine, sisters Christine and Alma in the backseat, and a cousin John on the running board

Clara Frykman

On March 31, 1915, **Clara Wilhelmina Johnson** married **Nels J. Frykman**, son of **Nels (Nils) and Christina (Stina) Frykman**. She, a distant cousin, was 28 and he was 44. The large farm was given to them as a wedding present from Nels John's parents. To this union two children, Mrs.

Haaken (Alice) Skarphol of Souris, N.D. and Alvin were born. (From Frykman Family History)

Her obituary in the *Grant County Herald* reported she was the daughter of John and Lena Johnson, and at the time of her death her brother Aldrich Johnson of Okeley and a sister Mrs. Arne Carlson of Akely.

Clara Wilhelmina was a sister to **Mrs. Peter Setterlund (Karin)**. Below is a picture of Nels J. and Clara courtesy of Allen Frykman.

Alvin and Clarice Frykman

Alvin Rudolph Frykman was born in Erdahl township September 18, 1917, to **Nels John and Clara (Johnson) Frykman**. He was baptized and confirmed at Zionsborg Lutheran Church. On October 21, 1945, he married **Clarice** Kolkind at the Immanuel Lutheran Church of Evansville. The couple was blessed with five children: Mary Eileen, Vivian Elaine, Dwayne Roger, Joyce Alyce, and Allen John.

He farmed the home farm, which was homesteaded by his grandparents, until 1970 when he rented out the farm land and began to haul gravel from the pit on the farm. In his early years he enjoyed working and farming with horses. He also worked at the Barrett Ice Works several winters. One of his hobbies was ice fishing; and his children fondly remember him clearing the ice on a pond, so they could skate.

In 1981 He and Clarice moved to Hoffman and in 1993 they moved to Evansville, where they were members of Faith Lutheran Church. Alvin loved his family and enjoyed spending time and playing dominos with his grandchildren and attending school events.

Alvin died May 22, 2000, at Crestview Manor Nursing Home in Evansville. Upon his death, he was survived by his wife Clarice, his five children-Mary (Reece) Lund of Evansville, Vivian (Richard) Spicer of Birmingham, Mich., Dwayne (Linda) Frykman of Rockwall, TX, Joyce (Mark) Hjelle of Fergus Falls and Allen (Michele)Frykman- 12 grandchildren and two great-grandchildren. He was preceded in death by his parents and sister, Alyce Skarphol. His funeral was held at Faith Lutheran Church with Rev. Irving Arnquist officiating. Music was provided by organist Dorothy Kammerer and vocalists Twyla Johnson, Marcia and Amber Quinn singing "His Eye is on the Sparrow." Casketbearers were Darrell Frykman, Douglas Frykman, David Frykman, Kenneth Person, Curtis Person, and Dayton Skarphol.

Clarice Frykman

"**Clarice Marjorie** Kolkind was born November 17, 1925 to Andrew and Adeline (Johnson) Kolkind near Evansville. She was baptized December 11, 1925 and confirmed May 19, 1940 at Immanuel Lutheran Church, Evansville.

Clarice married **Alvin** Frykman on October 21, 1945, at Immanuel Lutheran Church. Together they raised their family and farmed near Barrett. She worked at Runestone Telephone in Hoffman for 18 years where she became the office manager. In the early 1990's the couple moved into Evansville. **Alvin** passed away May 22, 2000. Clarice lived at Rolling Hills assisted living in Barrett from 2006 until February 2010 when she became a resident of Evansville Care Center. Clarice Frykman, age 85, of Evansville, died Tuesday, January 18, 2011 at Evansville Care Center.

Clarice was a lifetime member of Immanuel/Faith Lutheran Church. She was active in Ladies Aid and served as a Sunday school teacher. Clarice was also a 4-H leader. She enjoyed quilting, crocheting and traveling. Clarice especially enjoyed the couple's 40th anniversary trip to Norway and Sweden.

She is survived by her children, Mary (Reece) Lund of Evansville, Vivian (Richard) Spicer of Birmingham, MI, Dwayne (Connie) Frykman of Uvave, TX, Joyce (Mark) Hjelle of Fergus Falls, Allen (Michelle) Frykman of Elbow Lake; 12 grandchildren, Wendy Lund/Feltman, Kerby Lund, Richard Spicer Jr, Sean Spicer, Timothy Spicer, Kevin Spicer, Megan Spicer, Erik Hjelle, Kara Hjelle, Ross Hjelle, Andrea Frykman, Emily

Frykman; 6 great grandchildren, Kannen, Kennedy, Kerryn and Kiley Lund, Noah and Quinton Spicer; sister, Agnes Person of Elbow Lake; sister-in-law, Eleanor Kolkind of Isanti; many nieces, nephews, relatives and friends.

Clarice was preceded in death by her husband, Alvin; her parents; brother, Alvin Kolkind; and brother- in-law, Paul Person"(obituary from Glende-Nilson.com).

Her children's fond memories of Clarice were that she enjoyed working at the RTA very much and always did a lot of baking. It was always so nice to come home after school and smell the aroma of what was baked that day. As mentioned in the obituary, one of Clarice's hobbies was crocheting. Each grandchild received a hand crocheted afghan for graduation. In addition she made many quilts. (Information on Alvin and Clarice from daughter Mary and obituaries)

Per Nilsson Frykman

From Grandell Unger Family Tree. **Per Nilsson Frykman** was born December 26, 1844 to Nils and **Ingeborg** (Persdotter) Nilsson in Varmland, Sweden. He married Stina Petterson daughter of Jonas and Kirstie (Larsdotter) Petterson in Varmland. They immigrated to Minnesota in 1882 to Erdahl township where they homesteaded on Section 35 200 acres and farmed another 160 acres in section 34. They had five children: **John Per Frykman, Maria,** Ida (Booke), **Gerda** (Anderson), and Helena (Gustafson). Per was known as a rugged pioneer and honorable citizen. He died November 30, 1933, of Pydenephritis.

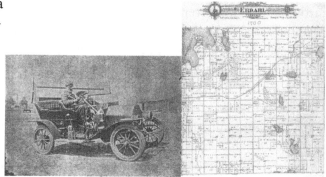

Stina Frykman

Stina Petterson daughter of Jonas and Kirstie Petterson was born December 22, 1837, in Sweden. She married **Per N. Frykman** in 1874 and immigrated to Minnesota in 1882 to Erdahl township where they homesteaded on Section 35 200 acres and farmed another 160 acres in section 34. (She was a younger sister of **Kristine (Nils Nilson Frykman)**. She died November 1, 1915, from complications of a fractured hip. Picture of Per and Stina 1911 from Zionsborg History Notes

John P. and Ida Frykman

John Preus Frykman was born January 8, 1879, to **Per Nils and Stina Frykman**. They immigrated to America in 1882. He married **Ida** Newhouse of Minneapolis at the Immanual Parsonage in Evansvillle on June 4, 1923, and they resided on the old **Per Frykman** farm. They had three children **Preus** and Martin and daughter **Stina Olivia**. He died August 5, 1959.

Ida Frykman

(From her obituary in the *Grant County Herald* October 3, 1974) "**Mrs. Ida Frykman**, 90, Elbow Lake, died last Tuesday at the Crest View Manor Nursing home at Evansville, where she has lived the past four years. Funeral services were held Friday at Bethlehem Lutheran church, Rev. Paul R. Peterson officiated. Burial was in Zionsborg cemetery, Evansville.

Organist was Mrs. Harold Mohagen. Soloist was Rev. Arthur Wickstrom. Pall bearers were Jule Elvrum, **Alvin, Bertil**, Darrell and Douglas Frykman and Orlando Jenstad. The daughter of Mr. and Mrs. Nyhus she was born May 25, 1884 in Trondhjem, Norway. She came to Barrett when she was 17 years old she lived there a short time and then moved to Minneapolis where she worked as a cook.

She was married to **John P. Frykman** June 6, 1923. They farmed in Erdahl township until 1948 when they moved to Willlmar. They lived there eight years before moving to Elbow Lake. .."

They had two sons—**Preus and Martin**—and a daughter Stina Olvia.

Stina Olivia Frykman

Stina was an infant daughter born to **J.P. and Ida Frykman**. As the headstone reads she was born and died in 1924.

Preus Frykman

(from Findagrave.com) "**Preus Frykman**, 75, of Elbow Lake, died Saturday, Dec. 16, 2000, at Lake Region Hospital in Fergus Falls.

He was born March 17, 1925, to **John and Ida (Nyhus) Frykman** and grew up in Erdahl Township. He graduated from Evansville High School in 1943, and on Sept. 1, 1946, married Doris Anderson. The couple settled east of Barrett where they started 40 years of dairy farming. He was also a Dekalb seed corn salesman. Mr. Frykman served on the Barrett School Board for 12 years, participated in the Grant County Barbershop Choir, was a treasurer and board member of the Zionsborg Lutheran Church and a board member of the joint churches in Barrett, and Erdahl Town Board. He enjoyed duck and pheasant hunting, particularly deer hunting in the fall with his fellow elite hunting party. He also enjoyed all seasons of fishing, especially sun fishing on Pelican. Throughout his retirement, he remained very involved and enjoyed all aspects of farming. He and his wife were active bowlers and committed to attending their children and grandchildren's many school and sporting events. Through the years, he also contributed his harmonious tenor voice in many beautiful solos at several events.

Survivors include his wife Doris; two sons, Doug (Marilyn) Frykman of Barrett and Darrell (Susan) Frykman of Elbow Lake; two daughters, Connie (Jim) Warde of Elbow Lake and Kris (Gary) Lien of Apple Valley; 13 grandchildren; four great-grandchildren; and one brother, Martin Frykman of Big Bear, Calif.

He was preceded in death by his parents; and an infant sister."

Peter Frykman Home Page

Peter Frykman married Hilma Christine Okerlund March 12, 1912. Peter bought the Okerlund farm, which was settled by John and Ellen (Bergerson) Okerlund. The Okerlunds started with a dugout along the Chippewa River and later built a house, barn, and other outbuilding. This is how the house, obviously added to over time, and one granary look in 2012.

Peter and Hilma Frykman

(from documents at the Evansville Historical Foundation) **Peter Frykman** was born January 2, 1873, in Fryksande, Varmland Sweden to **Nils and Britta Christina (Nilsson)Frykman**. His family immigrated to America in 1881 when he was only 8 years old. As a child he helped his brother and father cut wood. He attended school through fourth grade, and was confirmed in Zionsborg Church at the age of 16.

At the age of 23 he was working with his brother Nels threshing. He was feeding the machine by hand and accidently cut his right hand. "His uncle, Per Frykman drove the team of horses to take Peter to Dr. Hand in Elbow Lake, But after going a short distance, Peter said to his uncle, Per, 'I will drive the horses myself. There's no sense in killing them driving so fast.' His was slightly deformed from this accident. During the time he stayed in Elbow Lake recuperating he contracted typhoid fever.

He married Hilma Christine Okerlund March 12, 1912 at the home of Mr. and Mrs. Carl Borgrud with Reverend S. W. Swenson officiating. Her sister Olga and his brother Victor stood up for them. He worked with Oscar Malmgren doing stone masonry work.

They lived on the Okerlund farm and had two children, Earl Calvin Bertil and Isola (married Howard Johnson). Peter often told Bertil there were 'Lake-Water Finns' in the ancestry. At one time some Finns were brought to Varmland as mercenary solders for Russia. Some were brought as woodsmen. Peter was known as a kind and generous man. In the cold winter, he often gave the children a ride to school.

His wife died in 1931, and after that he 'lost his zest for living and died of pernicious anemia June 22, 1935, at the age of 62.'

Peter Frykman and Oscar Malmgren at work in Evansville

Hilma Frykman

(from documents at the Evansville Historical Foundation) Hilma was born February 19, 1876, to John (born Johannes Olsson in Vastra Hagvalta, Varmland, Sweden)and Ellen Okerlund in a dugout in the bank of Chippewa River on what is now the Frykman Century farm. Here they squatted in 1874 until they were able to purchase the land in 1878. Indians traveling by canoe visited the dugout to secure salt and bread. John and Ellen raised 12 children here. Hilma married **Peter Frykman** March 12, 1912, at the home of Mr. and Mrs. Carl Borgrud with Reverend S.

W. Swenson officiating. Her sister Olga and his brother Victor stood up for them.

He worked with **Oscar Malmgren** doing stone masonary work as well as thrashing and farming. Peter and his brother **John (Nels Johan)** had one of the early steam engine threshing rigs. Hilma was a seamstress and also worked in the millinery shop of Kate and Maude Knapton in Alexandria.

In 1913 Hilma and Peter (who lived only 4 miles west) took over the farm. Hilma and Peter had 2 children, **Bertil** and **Isola (Johnson)**. Aside from their home and farm, their main interest was the Zionsborg church.

Bertil and Ruth Frykman

Earl Calvin Bertil Frykman was born May 6, 1914 to **Peter and Hilma Christine (Okerlund) Frykman** in Douglas County Minnesota. "He was a baptized and confirmed member of the Zionsborg Lutheran church. He attended School district #26 and graduated from Evansville High school in 1931. [graduating salutatorian] He then attended Gustavus Adolphus College in St. Peter, MN. After working a short time at the Farmers State Bank he returned to farming due to his father's ill health. He ran the family farm until his retirement and moved into Evansville in 1983. He farm was named a Century Farm in 1976.

Bertil was active in community and church affairs, among the many boards he served on were the Rural School and Consolidated School District, Zionsborg, Immanuel and Faith Lutheran Church, the Knute Nelson Memorial Home and Zionsborg Cemetery.

He was married October 8, 1938, on a beautiful sunshiny [sic] day at St. Petri Lutheran Church to **Ruth** Shurson, daughter of Olaf and Clara Christenson Shurson of Brandon Township" (obituary from Nilson Funeral Home).

They had three children: David, **Neta (Lamp)**, and Richard. He died October 8, 1988 on the night of his 50th wedding anniversary.

In an interview (Sharon Saxton 1984- Evansville Historical Society document), Bertil said that his early childhood with his sister was quiet and secluded and as a teenager he stayed in town during the school week

with his aunt and uncle because they lived 10 miles out in the country. There is more on this and Ruth's interview at the Evansville Historical Foundation.

Ruth Frykman

"Ruth Frykman was born April 3, 1917 on the family farm in Evansville Township to Olaf and Clara (Christenson) Shurson. She was baptized and confirmed at St. Petri Lutheran Church. She attended rural District 32 and graduated from Brandon High School in 1933. Ruth then attended 1 year at the normal training department of the Alexandria High School. She worked for her room and board at a small home for Mrs. O.S. Larson. Ruth started teaching in rural school District No. 26 at the age of 17, where she taught for two years and she also taught for two years at District No. 32.

On October 8, 1938 she and **Bertil Frykman** were married at St. Petri Lutheran Church they lived on a Century Farm south west of Evansville where they raised 3 children. Off the farm interests were Zionsborg Church and Cemetery Association, Evansville Schools, 4-H Clubs, Douglas County Historical Society, Evansville Historical Foundation, and numerous community activities. When Zionsborg closed they joined Immanuel Church in Evansville which became Faith Lutheran Church of Evansville.

Ruth and Bertil farmed together for 45 years. In 1983 they sold the farm to their son David and retired in Evansville. Bertil died on their 50th Anniversary, October 8, 1988. At the present time Ruth lived in the Evansville Care Center.

After retirement they enjoyed traveling to many states, always happy to come home to Evansville, their church and friends. Ruth continued some traveling with friends and family after the death of Bertil - a highlight was the Oberammergau Passion Play in 1990 and travels in Central Europe and Scandinavia.

Ruth is survived by David Frykman, Evansville, MN; **Neta Lamp**, Newbery Park, CA; Richard (Carol) Frykman, New Prague, MN; grandchildren: Lorena (Robert) Caulfield and their children Luke, Clara and Alexa, Newbery Park, CA; Jeremiah (Telma) Rees and their children Ondria and Nicole, Glendora, CA; Jon (Alicia) Frykman, Hutchinson, MN; Paul (Angie) Frykman, Duluth, MN."

She was preceded in death by her husband Bertil and grandson Brian Frykman. She died May 17, 2011." (findagrave.com)

Rudolph and Esther Hansen

Born November 21, 1904 to Hans and Kathrine Hansen (both of Danish descent) in Kingsbury County, South Dakota, was **Rudolph Christian Hanson**. He was the third of six children: Avold, Nels, Rudolph, Olga, Lillian, and Anna.

March 15, 1928, he married **Esther L. Nelson** in Oldham, South Dakota. They set up house in Whitewood township, Kingsbury County, South Dakota where their first child Dorothy was born. They went on to moved to Urness township, Douglas county (on the **Nils Aldrin** farm) and have four more children: Harold, Arland, Beverly, and Barbara. Barbara was born after the other children had grown and moved away and became the "apple of Daddy's eye."

As a farmer, Rudolph worked hard, especially milking his cows and tending to the field work. This left little time for any hobby or recreation. Although he enjoyed fishing.

Rudolph died 1977. (information from Beverly Nelson, daughter)

Esther Hanson

Esther Leila was born January 3, 1905, in Carthage, South Dakota, to Eric Nicolai and Bertha (Stordahl) Nelson. She had five other siblings: Gertrude, Tilde, Donald, Mary, Linol.

March 15, 1928, she married **Rudolph Hanson** in Oldham, South Dakota. They set up house in Whitewood township, Kingsbury County, South Dakota where their first child Dorothy was born. They went on to moved to Urness township, Douglas county (on the **Nils Aldrin** farm) and have four more children: Harold, Arland, Beverly, and Barbara.

Esther was a busy housewife and co-worker on their farm. She always had a big garden and raised chickens. Esther also enjoyed fishing. Beverly remembers Esther made a cement little fish pond in the backyard and stocked it with gold fish. There was a little foot bridge that crossed the pond and the cat would love to sit there and "watch" the fish. (information from Beverly Nelson, daughter)

Doug Alvstad's favorite memory of Esther was her home-grown popcorn. When the Alvstads played whist at the Hanson home, Esther served popcorn. Even though Doug thought it was great, the Hanson kids remember the hand shucking as a memory they would like to forget.

Esther died February 17, 1997, in Evansville.

Beatrice Hickey

Born March- 1890 to **Charles G. and Christianna Peterson**. Beatrice Mertina was one of seven children. Her siblings were **Euphemia, baby, Capitola** (Barron), Carl, Cecil, and **Vivian** (Sowers). In 1912 she married W.C. Hickey of Everett, Washington. Beatrice lived in Canada until 1922. She died August 19, 1937. She was a cousin to Mrs. C.V. Ostrom. (information from Douglas County obituary file listing *The Evansville Enterprise*, September 2, 1937 as the source.

Ole, Marit, Mary and Anne Jenstad

Ole, wife Marit, and daughter Anna are buried under this tree in unmarked graves. Ernest Franzen was their son-in-law.

Ole and Marit Jenstad

Ole G. Jenstad was born at Sundalen, Norway, September 29, 1847, to Gunder and Anna Jenstad. According to *The History of Douglas and Grant Counties*, His siblings included Haugen and Olava, who both died in Norway. Ole married **Marit** "Mary" Halvorsdatter. They immigrated to America in 1882. He worked as a farm hand and was employed by the railroad. In 1890 they moved onto the homeplace and in 1894 he purchased the 120 acres in Elk Lake township. They had four children—**Anna**, Gunder, **Mary, and Hilda**. The first three were born in Norway.

"He has always been an advocate of good roads and of the best of schools, and has served as a member of the school board and as a road boss. He has always had the confidence and the respect of the community and is highly regarded by all who know him." Marit died in July 23, 1899. He died March 19, 1924, after an illness of about two weeks. According to his obituary his death was caused by a stomach ailment. He was a faithful member of Zionsborg. His pallbearers were N.J. Frykman, Oscar Malmgren, Hjalmar Malmgren and Johnnie Peterson.

Anne Jenstad

Anna died at the age of nine in a fire.

Mary Jenstad

Mary born in Norway July 18, 1881. She lived most of her life on her family farm in Elk Lake Township, first with her parents and siblings, then with her sister and husband, and finally with her brother-in-law after her sister died. Mary died September 25, 1954.

John and Ellen Johnson

John Johnson was born in 1834 in Sweden. He immigrated in 1867 and married **Ellen** in 1886. Ellen was born in 1847 and died 1929. In 1900, the census shows him(66) with two children, **Albert** and **Emil**. He and Ellen farmed in Evansville township , section 31, just east of Lake Albert. (Also the 1900 census shows **John Swenson** living with the Johnsons. Coincidentally, John Swenson's daughter **Jennie** and her husband **Martin T. Martin** bought the Johnson homestead.)

Ellen Johnson

Ellen was born in Norway in November 1847 and immigrated to the US in 1880 or 1881. She married John Johnson in 1886 and had 2 children, **Albert** and **Emil**.

Emil Hjalmer
Emil Hjalmer was born January 19, 1890 and died October 31, 1917, at the age of only 27.

Albert and Vera Johnson

The Park Region Echo, December 9, 1965, "**Albert J. Johnson** Last Rites Held..Albert Julius Johnson born Oct. 27, 1887 in Evansville, Minn., the son of John and Ellen Johnson.

"In June, 1920, he was married to **Vera** V. Bartlett of Alexandria. The family moved to Alexandria 15 years ago.

"Mr. Johnson died Nov. 16, 1965 at the age of 78 years and 20 days...

"He is survived by his widow, Mrs. Vera Johnson, six children: Allen Milke of Seattle Wash., Louis Milke of Bremerton, Wash., Mrs. Eunice Svee of St. Cloud, Julius Johnson of Everrett, Wash., Herbert Johnson of Minneapolis and Flora Mae (Mrs. James Olson) of Alexandria. Also surviving are 12 grandchildren and six great grandchildren."

"He was preceded in death by one brother and one son."

Vera Johnson

Vera was born in Desmet, South Dakota, on September 22, 1886, the daughter of Ally and Eva (Butmann) Bartlett. She moved to the Alexandria-Evansville area at the age of 14, according to her obituary. In the 1920 Census, she is listed as divorced with two children Ally (Allen) and Lewis living with her parents in Hudson Township south of Alexandria.

She married **Albert Johnson**, son of **John and Ellen Johnson**, in 1920. They moved to Evansville and moving to Alexandria in 1949 after retiring. They had 5 children Herbert, **Emil**, Julius, Eunice, and Mrs. (Flora Mae) James Olson. Emil died in infancy.

Emil Johnson

Emil was the infant son of **Albert and Vera Johnson** born and died in 1923 at the age of 2 months old. He is buried in an unmarked grave on the east side of his grandparents' graves.

Howard and Isola Johnson

Howard was born April 21, 1917, in Alexandria to Clarence and Matilda Evenson Johnson of Brandon. According to information found at the Evansville Historical Foundation, he was a draftsman and made estimates for a lumber yard and several houses. He graduated from high school and also from the Minnesota School Business in Minneapolis. He served with the U.S. Army during World War II (1942-1945). Following his discharge, he married 18 April 1944 Isola Frykman. They had 2 children Kathryn and James Peter.

He managed lumber yards at Spring Valley, WI, Heron Lake, Springfield and Thief River Falls. He was employed by Tomlinson Lumber Company at Callaway. The Johnsons moved to Detroit Lakes in 1972. He was an active member and past president of Viking Land Lodge No. 495, Sons of Norway. He loved music, was a choir member and could fill in for the band if a drummer was needed. He loved concerts, and was a barbershop singing member (bass soloist). He was active in the church (worship and music committees and council member). If there is any spare time, he also liked the read. They had always enjoyed having a dog in their home. He died in Detroit Lakes September 13, 1989.

Howard C. Johnson

Photos courtesy of Evansville Historical Foundation

Isola Johnson

Born July 28, 1916, to **Peter and Hilma (Okerland)Frykman**. Her full name was Isola Ellen Christine.She was baptized and confirmed at Zionsborg. She grew up with her brother **Bertil** on the family farm just north of Lake Albert. She attended rural School district 26 for eight years and graduated from Evansville High School in 1934. According to information found at the Evansville Historical Society, she was housekeeper in a large motel for 12 years. [Edgewater Condominiums from 1972-1988] She was an active church worker. She graduated from high school and was a Beauty Culture graduate, and worked at this for many years before her marriage.

She married **Howard C. Johnson** April 18, 1944. She wore a heart shaped locket, a gift of the groom, and a brooch her mother wore at her wedding 31 years before. They had 2 children Kathryn Christine born April 7, 1946, and James Peter born January 2, 1954.

She enjoyed plants and had them all over their home and Howard's workroom. She also enjoyed working with wood and loved to go rock hunting. She had many beautiful collections of rocks inside and outside their home. She died November 21, 2001 in Detroit Lakes, MN.

Vallence Jones

Vallence Lester Jones was born February 15, 1909 and died February 22, 1909. He was born to Olof and Pauline Jones in Erdahl Township. Olof and Pauline had eight other children: Helen, Harald O., Ina Rubin Walton, Vernon, May Pauline (Polly), and Robert.

Olof and Pauline (Paulina Ostrom) were from Skane Lan, Sweden. Olof born in 1871 or 1872 to Jens Jones and Bengte Jensen. He immigrated to America in 1890. Olof and Pauline were married in 1897. Before moving to Erdahl, they lived in New Sweden, Nicolett, MN; and after Vallence's death, they must have left Erdahl Township and moved to Isanti, MN, where they were recorded living in 1920 Census. Olof was self employed and died December 8, 1951, in Princeton Township, Mille Lacs, MN. Pauline died in 1950 and buried in Mt. Pleasant Cemetery near Onamia. Most of the information for this bio was taken from the Census and Olof's death record from the Church of Latterday Saints ancestry research internet site www.familysearch.org. and www.findagrave. com .

Neta Lamp

"**Neta Marie Frykman** was born February 7, 1942, in Alexandria, MN, to **Bertil and Ruth Frykman**. She was the middle child with two brothers, David and Richard. Neta was baptized and confirmed at Zionsborg Lutheran Church. She graduated from Evansville High School in 1960. She also attended Gustavus Adolphus college at St. Peter and was a nursing Major graduating 1964.

As a child she was in 4-H and school activities. She became interested in the Peace Corp, which had just started in 1962, and in June of 1964 she joined 10 nurses and about 25-30 others who went to do community

work in Chile. She was stationed in Valdivia, Chile, where they set up inoculations of rural populations against small pox. There she met her first husband Fernando Rees, a native Chilean. She and her first husband returned to the U.S. in 1967. They lived in Evansville briefly, then in Los Angeles, where she worked at a Catholic hospital, the oldest in LA. She completed her masters degree in nursing at UCLA, and worked as a nursing supervisor at several hospitals including Cedar's Sinai Medical Center, Anaheim Memorial, St Vincent's, Medical Center, and Barlow Community Hospital.

She had two children Jeremy and Lorena (Caulfied). She later divorced. She remarried Ed Lamp. They loved to travel and purchased a sailing boat and cabin on Bois Blanc Island in Michigan. They took several trips in the US and around the world, including a safari in Africa, on the Orient Express from Beijing, China to St. Peterburg, Rusia and even spent NewYear's Eve in Antarctica.

Neta battled cancer for 15 months and died shortly after her second husband, June 15, 2011, in Newbury Park, California." (Evansville Historical Foundation)

Gladys Adele Lawrence

"Gladys, the youngest of five children, was born on February 21, 1918 to **John and Mathilda** (Lindstrom) **Swenson** near Evansville, MN. She attended rural grade school in School District 49, while growing up on the family farm in Urness Township. She was baptized and confirmed in Zionsborg Lutheran Church, south of Evansville. While she was growing up she recalled the long trek to school, crossing pastures and being careful to look out for the bull that would frequently chase her and her siblings. Many years later she still recalled vivid dreams of being chased by that same bull. She also remembered the cold winters, carrying baked potatoes in their mittens in order to keep themselves warm.

She received her beautician's license after attending school in Minneapolis, Minn., while living with her sister, **Jennie Martin**.

Gladys married Charles J. Lawrence on Nov. 18, 1938 in Wahpeton, N.D. They were blessed with a beautiful family of four children, C. David, Richard, Andrea, and Cynthia. Past employment included Melby Studio of Photography and a cook at St. Francis Nursing Home. On Sept. 10, 1968, while working at St. Francis Home, she earned her G.E.D., an accomplishment she was very proud of. She enjoyed caring for her garden of roses and wildflowers; an interest rekindled from when she enjoyed the wildflowers near their home while growing up. She would walk to mailbox to collect the mail, often gathering bouquets of flowers along the way.

Gladys was a member of Breckenridge Lutheran Church and her deep faith in God and love for her family helped sustain her through the years. Gladys was a wonderful cook and loved it whenever her family gathered together and she could prepare her delicious 'food from the heart.' She also was an avid reader of Louis L'Amour books and painted flowers and landscapes with oils and acrylics. Her many works of art are cherished by family and friends.

Gladys passed away on October 16, 2012, at the age of 94. She is buried beside her father and mother, John and Mathilda Swenson.

Gladys' family has many good memories involving Zionsborg Lutheran Church while growing up and visiting the homes of their aunts and uncles in the Evansville area. They remember with great fondness the church functions including dinners, attending church services and Sunday School in which their aunt, Helen Clow, taught classes." (pictures and story submitted by Cynthia Krier)

Gladys is survived by her children Charles David (Marlene) Lawrence of Ivanhoe, Minn., Andrea (Charles) Kohoutek of Rapid City, S.D. and Cynthia (Ronald) Krier of Breckenridge; her daughter-in-law Ann Lawrence; 14 grandchildren and 21 great- grandchildren; and many nieces and nephews who loved her very much.

Gladys was preceded in death by her parents; her husband; her son Richard Michael and three sisters — **Helen Clow,** Alice Strand and **Jennie Martin**; and her brother Alden Swenson.

John Lindstrom Home Page

John (Johan) Lindstrom was born February 28, 1815. He was 53 years old when he emigrated from Sweden to Minnesota. He filed for his homestead on November 9, 1876, in section 4 of Urness Township. He and his second wife Martha "mortgaged this land , but paid it off. He also bought property for Ole O. Kierkjordan and Aseneth M. Smith. In 1886, he appears to have owned—free of mortgage –310 acres in section 4 of Urness Township." (family history Evansville Historical Foundation)

John Lindstrom

John (Johan) Lindstrom was born February 28, 1815 and died May 24, 1896. He was 53 years old when he emigrated from Sweden to Minnesota. He came to America on the City of New York July 1868. His first wife is thought to be Karin Jonsdotter -66, who was listed just below his name on the manifest. Also listed is Gertrude Jonsdotter-21, their daughter, who later married a Mr. Johnson. Karin or Kari died July 25, 1871. Their daughter **Marit** (Mrs. **Erick Nelson**) was born in 1843.They had one son Lars Lindstrom (father of **Mathilda Swenson**) who also immigrated in 1868. The site of Kari's grave is unknown; however, there were two or three graves at the south end of the Lars Lindstrom property, one which may be hers, the other two are assumed to be Jennie Lindstrom, who died of tuberculosis in 1899 and one a stillborn baby of Maria's .

John homestead in Section 4 of Urness Township. By 1886 he owned 400 acres in Urness Township. This would have been a quite large land holding during this time period.

July 27, 1872, he married **Martha** Andersdotter (also known as Anderson). She had three children before this union—Christine, **Fritz**, and Caroline. They were charter members of Zionsborg Church.

"There is little additional information concerning John or Martha...It's very impressive that someone who had come to the U.S. at the age of 53, probably with little or no knowledge of English, and with little money, could have accumulated such an estate within 25 years."

John became incompetent and in 1893, his grandson Nils J. Lindstrom was appointed guardian. His property was inventoried and valued at $6,761 (a goodly amount in those days). John died three years later at the age of 81. (information from the family history by Carolyn Townsend.)

Martha Lindstrom

Martha has no separate headstone but is buried on this lot with John

Martha Andersdotter or Anderson, who married **John Lindstrom** July 27, 1872, appears to have had three children prior to her marriage. They are Christine Lindstrom (1875 census), Fritz "Fritzoph Jangsoth," and Caroline Nelson, (1880 census)-Carolina married John Gustafson and also died in Souris, Bottineau County.

According to the Lindstrom Branch of the Erickson/Lindstrom family history, after Karin's death, "John met a woman named Martha Anderson...who had been born in Sweden in May of 1829. She had emigrated [sic] to Goodhue County and, from there, to Douglas County in 1870. On July 27, 1872 –one year and two days after Karin's death—John and Martha were married.

John's family did not approve of this marriage. Martha was 14 years his junior and she had three children: a 16-year old, a 5- year, and a new baby. John's financial responsibilities were suddenly and considerably increased and, at that time, he was probably considered 'old.' But perhaps his family didn't realize that-- despite his age—his needs for human companionship were not unlike their own. Martha provided comfort and companionship and, with her children, a family. They gave John good reason(s) to work and earn and look forward to 'tomorrow.' They also saved Lars and Maria (his nearest relatives) from having to worry over, cook for, care for, and listen to a lonely, aging man..."She died at the age of 70.

Fritz Lindstrom Home Page

Fritz Lindstrom moved with his mother and two sisters to Urness Township, where his mother married John Lindstrom.

In 1901, Fritz purchased a 320 acre farm, named Meadow Lawn, in Section 33, Evansville Township where he lived with his wife and raised his family. He purchased the acres from Berut Anseth . In 1948 when he retired and bought a home in Evansville. (below house SW view and barn in 1914 from Edith Lang and Carol Day)

Fritz and Carrie Lindstrom

Fritz Lindstrom, pioneer citizen and charter member of Zionsborg Lutheran Church, was born March 10, 1867 in Goodhue County; his mother was **Martha** Andersdotter (also known as Anderson) father unknown. Christine, **Fritz**, and Caroline. The family moved from Goodhue County to Douglas County in 1870. She married **John Lindstrom** July 27, 1872. The Census of 1875 lists the children as Christine Lindstrom 19, born in Sweden, Fritjoph (Fritz) Jangsoth, 8, born in Minnesota, and Carolina Wilsen (actually Nilson or Nelson), 3, born in Minnesota. In 1880 they were listed as Christine Nelson, Fritz Nelson, and Gustava C. (Carolina)Nelson. It can be assumed that Martha was married before and widowed. Christine kept the name Nelson. Fritz and Carolina took the Lindstrom name as their own.

Carolina (Lena)married John Gustafson and she and Christine died in Souris, ND. (a number of families left this area for Souris when land was opened by the railroad companies.) Fritz remained here. He and his parents were Charter members of Zionsborg.

According to a family bio submitted by Edith Lang-Ogden and her sister Carol Day (granddaughters) " Fritz Lindstrom, pioneer citizen and charter member of Zionsborg Lutheran Church, moved with his family when he was 3 to a farm in Urness Township Douglas County, MN. [see **John Lindstrom**]

In 1901, he purchased a farm in Section 33, Evansville Township where he lived until 1948 when he retired and bought a home in Evansville. He died at the age of 85 years old on May 31, 1952.

Fritz married **Karin (Carrie)** Borg in St. Paul on November 19, 1896. The couple celebrated their golden anniversary at an event in Zionsborg Church in 1946. At that time he was the only living charter member of Zionsborg Church.

There were 5 children in the Lindstrom family: Nannie (Mrs. John Norgren), Arthur (Alice Peterson), **Ruth** who died at the age of 17, **Robert** (Nina Carlson and **Emilie** Bartelt) and Thelma (Mrs. Joubert Johnson).

The Lindstrom farm included 320 acres. The Chippewa River, where Fritz spent time fishing, ran through the farm. At the time that farmers were encouraged to name their farm, the name "Meadow Lawn" was chosen. A new large home was built for the family about 1913. A windpowered generator provided electricity long before REA came through. Fritz took good care of his horses but he never drove a tractor. He did drive a car, his last one being a 1927 Chevrolet which he continued to drive through the 1940s. Fritz had a respect-a reverence-for the land. On

Sunday afternoons, he 'walked the fields' checking progress of the crops, noting the wildlife along the river and making sure pasture fences were in good condition."

Carrie Lindstrom

"**Carrie** was born Karin Borg in Gunnarskog, Varmland, Sweden, September 26, 1865, to Jon Borg and his wife Kajsa Andersdotter Borg. She was the second of seven children. [sister was **Martha Erickson –Ole's** wife] Carrie was baptized and confirmed in a Swedish Lutheran church. She came to America with her mother, sisters, and her brother in 1885. Her father and an older sister Marta came the year before and established a home near Melby. The family traveled in steerage class as most emigrants did. Kajsa was seasick during the trip and Carrie was responsible for the care of her younger siblings.

Carrie worked as a "hired girl" in Evansville homes and learned how homes in America were managed. Later, she was employed at the Geneva Beach Hotel and Letson House in Alexandria. By working in situations where English was spoken, she learned to understand and speak the language. In the same manner, she learned to read and write the English language. Carrie also worked as a dressmaker in St. Paul. This was at a time when ladies hired seamstresses to sew their clothing and before ready-to-wear clothing was available in stores. She married **Fritz Lindstrom** November 19, 1896. They made their home on the family farm in Urness Township until 1901 when they purchased a half section of land in Sec-

tion 33, Evansville Township. This was their home until they retired and moved to Evansville in 1946. [She and Fritz had five children— Thelma, **Robert**, Nannie, Arthur, and **Ruth**.] They farmed until 1946 when they moved into Evansville.

Carrie was a capable, independent, hard-working lady. In addition to the usual household work, she kept a big garden, raised chickens and sold eggs, churned cream and sold butter, and spun wool and knitted stockings, mittens and scarves for the family. In the days when the minister made the long trip by horse and buggy or cutter from Evansville to Zionsborg and Fryksande

Churches to conduct Sunday services, he was a welcome guest at their home for dinner and rest for both the pastor and his horse. Her well-tended garden provided much food for the family table. It was a matter of pride for her to have creamed new potatoes and peas for the annual Fourth of July picnic.

She had a sharp temper and did not tolerate bad behavior in her children and grandchildren. If you sat beside her at church, good behavior was rewarded with pink peppermint candy. Improper behavior resulted in a quick trip outside with suitable punishment and a fast return to the service. In the days when men sat on one side of church and women on the other, it was customary for the men to cross the aisle and give their spouse a dime to put in the collection plate. Not so for Carrie! She had her own money for the offering, saved from selling eggs or butter. Carrie believed in the value of education for her children. All of them attended country school in Districts 49 and/or 26. Nannie took the Normal Training course for teachers and also attended Moorhead Normal School (now MMSU). Arthur, Robert, and Thelma graduated from Northwestern College in Fergus Falls. She was a diligent worker in her church in the Ladies Aid, and the Missionary Society and in the Sunday School. The annual potato sausage supper at Zionsborg each fall was a Swedish feast enjoyed by many from the surrounding community." (submitted by Edith Lang and Carol Day, granddaughters)

"She became ill with pneumonia on New Year's Day and was taken to Wright's Memorial hospital at Fergus Falls on January 3. She recovered from this illness but old age and a weakened heart contributed to her death on January 31 at the age of 85." (from her obituary)

LEFT: Carrie with Fritz & grandkids

CENTER: The Children of Fritz and Carrie-Arthur , Ruth, Robert, Nanny, and Thelma.

RIGHT: Carrie with grandchild

Ruth Emilia Lindstrom

"**Ruth Lindstrom**, daughter of **Fritz and Carrie** Borg Lindstrom, was born on February 15, 1900, in Urness Township. She grew up in this neighborhood and died at the family home in Evansville Township on April 14, 1917.

She was never very strong and died of complications resulting from scarlet fever. She was remembered for her patience, cheerfulness and appreciation for those around her during her long illness.

Her funeral was held at Zionsborg Church on April 18, 1917, with Rev. Swenson giving an impressive sermon. He spoke of her work at the church where she played the organ for Sunday School. The choir sang her favorite songs and the Sunday School sang 'Jesus Loves Me, This I Know.'

Her survivors included her parents, an older sister Nannie (Mrs. John Norgren), her younger sister Thelma, and brother Arthur and Robert." (submitted by Edith Lang and Carol Day, daughters of Nannie and John Norgren)

ABOVE LEFT: Hilma Johnson and Ruth Lindstrom Confirmation. ABOVE RIGHT: Family picture back Robert and Ruth August 2, 1914 front Nannie, Arthur, and Thelma Pictures submitted by Edith Lang and Carol Day

Robert Walfred and "Millie" Emelie Lindstrom

"**Robert Lindstrom** was born on January 28, 1902, to Fritz and Car-

rie (Borg) Lindstrom. He grew up on the family farm in Evansville Township. He made his home on this farm for most of his life except for a few years in the village of Evansville.

Robert attended school in District 26 and graduated from Northwestern College in Fergus Falls. On July 8, 1931, he was united in marriage to Nina Carlson of Clitherall, also a graduate of Northwestern College. An extensive auto trip to the Black Hills followed their wedding. The couple made their home on the Lindstrom farm. Nina died on September 30, 1932, at the age of 31.

Robert continued to farm with his parents until their retirement . He moved with them to Evansville where he operated the Standard Service Station for a few years.

On October 19, 1952, he was united in marriage to Emilie Bartelt of Carlos, MN. The couple returned to the Lindstrom farm where they lived until his death on September 19, 1972. His funeral was held at the Faith Lutheran Church in Evansville on September 22, 1972, with Rev. Marvin Moll, clergyman, officiating.

Cars and tractors were important to Robert. In 1934, he, along with some friends, drove to the Chicago Worlds Fair. He owned an early Farmall tractor and a threshing machine and operated a 'threshing run' with his neighbors.

Robert enjoyed music and played the violin and a baritone. When a band was started at Evansville High School in 1937, he and Milton strand, who played the cornet, added their talent to the beginning band at basketball games and concerts. He also played the baritone in Community Band for many years.

Trapping along the Chippewa River and hunting deer in northern Minnesota were a big part of Robert's life. On one of these trips, he shot a black bear. The pelt was made into a beautiful rug. It frightened some

of the young nieces and nephews while others found it to be a good prop for imaginary expeditions." (bio. and pictures submitted by Edith Lang and Carol Day, daughters of Nannie and John Norgren)

PHOTOS AT LEFT: Robert as a baby and at age 14

PHOTOS NEXT PAGE: First marriage:Edwin Carlson, Robert and Nina(Carlson) and his sister Nannie. Second Marriage to Millie. (EHF)

Emilie "Millie" B. Lindstrom

Millie B. Lindstrom, age 96, of Parkers Prairie, died Wednesday, July 28, 2010, at St. William's Living Center in Parkers Prairie. Funeral services were held 1:30 p.m., Monday, August 2, 2010, at the chapel in St. William's Living Center in Parkers Prairie with Rev. Elton A. Hallauer officiating.

Emilie "Millie" Bertha Lindstrom was born July 10, 1914, to Albert and Olga (Ott) Bartelt in Belview, Minnesota. She was baptized July 26, 1914, at Peace Evangelical Lutheran Church in Echo, Minnesota. When she was two years old, her family moved to a farm near Carlos where she attended District #30 Country School through the eighth grade. She was confirmed on June 17, 1928, at Immanuel Lutheran Church in Carlos. She helped on the farm, did housekeeping for various families and worked in Reuter's and Kloehn's grocery stores in Carlos. She was united in marriage to **Robert Lindstrom** on October 19, 1952, at Immanuel Lutheran Church in Carlos. Following their marriage they lived in Evansville where they farmed and she taught Sunday school at Zionsborg Lutheran Church and belonged to its Ladies Aid. According to Edith Lang and

77

Carol Day, nieces, Millie "was famous for her delicious sponge cakes. She also enjoyed sewing, handwork, and gardening. She was a kind and caring person with a good sense of humor." Her husband, Robert died in September of 1972. A year later, she moved to Parkers Prairie where she lived in her own home until 2007, when she became a resident of St. William's Living Center. She was a member of Peace Evangelical Lutheran Church. She especially enjoyed sewing, handwork and gardening. (from her obituary) Photo courtesy Evansville Historical Foundation

Carl Lundblad

Carl Lundblad was born in Varmland, Sweden, July 27, 1876 to unknown and Lena Mattson Lundblad. Carl's father died in an accident. His mother and children were sent for by **John Johnson** of Erdahl township. She was a half sister to John's friend **Nils Aldrin**. They married and lived in Erdahl township. Carl died November 20, 1907. His headstone reads:

CARL JOHAN LUNDBLAD Born 27 July 1876, Died 20 November 1907, Dearly loved, deeply missed.

Malmgren Home Page

In 1880, Erik Frederick and Anna Beatrice (Strand) Malmgren moved to Erdahl township in Grant County, where he purchased land and farmed until his death. The house had additions as the family grew. This is how the house looked when Edwin Hoppe lived there. They had the house torn down and another moved on. Some of the stone foundation still remains.

Erik F. and Anna "Betsey" Malmgren

Erik Frederick Malmgren was born in Varmland Sweden, November 23, 1845, to Erik Petter and Johanna Sahlstrom Malmgren. According to his obituary (Grant County Historical), he came to America in the spring of 1868 and took up residence in Minneapolis. In July 14, 1871, he married Anna Beatrice "**Betsey**" Strand. They moved to Jordan, Minnesota, where Axel Victor, **Oscar** and **Charles** were born.

In 1880, he and his family moved to Erdahl township in Grant County, where he purchased land and farmed until his death. Here their family grew with the addition of Amelia, Johanna, **Eric Hjalmer**, **Hulda**, Hilma, Olga, and **Tilda**. In addition, they lost an **infant son** and Adolph N. Malmgren born and buried in 1890. The 1900 census showed that Erik and Betsey had 13 children, 10 of which were living. One can only assume that the other infant was born and died when they lived in Minneapolis or Jordan.

He and Betsey were charter member of Zionsborg Church. He was also active in the work of the township and county. He was a member of the board of the county commissioners for several terms. His obituary states, "He was a man who was pleasant to meet, neighborly, and well informed. Even the handicap of increasing age did not seem to deter him from his usual tireless activity." He died September 14, 1916, of heart failure.

Betsey Malmgren

Anna Beatrice's maiden name was Strand. This is evidenced in her obituary (Grant Co. Historical) and from death notices of some of her children, where their mother's maiden name was listed as Strand. She was born in Sweden July 14, 1851 and immigrated to America in 1869. At the time of her death she still had a brother living in Sweden. In July 14, 1871, she married Erik F. Malmgren in Minneapolis. They moved to Jordan, Minnesota, where Axel Victor, **Oscar** and **Charles** were born.

In 1880, they moved to Erdahl township in Grant County, where he purchased land and farmed until his death. Here their family grew with the addition of Amelia, Johanna, Eric Hjalmer, Hulda, Hilma, Olga, and

Tilda. In addition, they lost an **infant son** and **Adolph N. Malmgren** born and buried in 1890. The 1900 census showed that Erik and Betsey had 13 children, 10 of which were living. One can only assume that the other infant was born and died when they lived in Minneapolis or Jordan.

Betsey and Erik were charter members of Zionsborg Church. According to her obituary, they "went through the hardships of pioneering with the other old settlers. They raised a fine family and lived a happy, peaceful, and prosperous life." Betsey suffered a stroke in July and another just a week before her death. She died September 22, 1929, at the age of 78.

Adolph N. Malmgren and infant son

Two sons were born to Erick and Betsy Malmgren, who didn't live even a year. One is listed as only infant son (no date) and the other Adolph Nikaner (1890-1890)

Charles F. Malmgren

Charles F. Malmgren was the son of **Erik Fredrick and Betsy Malmgren**.

"Charles Malmgren, Charley, as he was called was born at Jordan, Minn., May 12, 1878. Later the family came to Erdahl township where Charley grew up on the farm now owned by the Edwin Hoppe family. He was confirmed in Zionsborg church June 23, 1895 by the late Rev. M.A. Nordstrom. His parents passed away many years ago, also his brothers, **Oscar** and Victor, and one sister **Hulda**. Some years ago they moved onto a small farm near Alexandria where he together with his brother, Hjalmer, and sister, Tillie, lived. Charley had surgery in May and recovered from that and was getting along fairly well. On Tuesday evening he quietly stepped out of his life..." (*Grant Co. Herald* Oct. 31, 1957)

EricH. Malmgren

Eric H. Malmgren was the son of **Erik Fredrick and Betsy Malmgren**. "Funeral services for Eric Hjalmer Malmgren were held Saturday, April 16 at 1:30 p.m. from the Zionsborg Lutheran church. The Rev. Marshall Gante officiated. Preus Frykman sang "Abide With Me" and "The Old Rugged Cross," accompanied by Mrs. Emma Fedje...

"Erick Hjalmer Malgren was born at Erdahl on January 26, 1882 the son of Eric F. and Beatrice Malgren. He was baptized and confirmed in the Zionsborg Lutheran church and attend school at District 47 in Grant County.

"Mr. Malgren passed away on Wednesday, April 13, at the age of 78 years, three months and 17 days..." (*Grant Co. Herald* April 21, 1960)

Hulda Malmgren

Hulda Malmgren was the daughter of **Erik and Betsy Malmgren**. She was born October 26, 1883 and died September 16, 1908.

Oscar Malmgren

"The Erdahl and surrounding communities were saddened last Saturday evening Sep, 19, (1942), when the news spread that **Oscar N. Malmgren** had passed away suddenly. He had worked in the fields that day and had returned home at night, apparently in good health, but while putting the horses in the barn he fell dead.

"Oscar Nikolaus Malmgren was born in Jordan, on August 17, 1875, and was the son **of Erick and Betsy Malmgren**. He has been a resident of Erdahl township since 1880, at which time his parents settled on the farm now known as the Malmgren farm. He never married but made his home with his brothers Hjalmer and Charles and his sister Tillie on the home farm.

"Mr. Malgren was an honored and respected citizen of his community and was a charter member of the Zionsborg Evangelical Lutheran church. He served for many years as a Deacon in his church, and has held other positions of responsibility in church and community.

"Those who immediately mourn his passing are his brothers, Victor Malmgren, Elbow Lake, and **Hjalmar** and **Charles** at the home farm in Erdahl township, and his sisters, Mrs. E. Gullifer (Anna), St. Paul, Mrs. V. Bloomquist (Amelia), Minneapolis, Mrs. A. Low (Hilma) Portland Ore., Mrs. El Olson (Olga), St. Paul, and **Tillie** at home..." (*Grant Co Herald* Sep 23, 1942)

Tillie Malmgren

"**Tillie Malmgren** was born in Erdahl Township October 14, 1894 to the late **Erick and Beatrice Malmgren** and grew to womanhood there on the farm... she attended school in District 47. She was baptized and confirmed in Zionsborg Lutheran Church and was a life long member there. After the death of her brother **Oscar**, they sold the farm, she and her brother **Charley and Hjalmer**, and bought a small farm near Alexandria. After the death of her two brother, she continued to make it her home until her health failed. She passed away from cancer at the Douglas County Hospital on December 21, at the age of 67 years...(*Grant Co. Herald* January 4, 1962)

Charles Lee Martin

"Charles Lee Martin was born August 15, 1954 to Robert and Harriet (Pearson) Martin in Alexandria, Minnesota. He had three other siblings: James, Charlene (Jennings) Waddingham, and Kristi (Huck). He attended elementary and high school at Evansville, MN. He married Debra Satterlie and they had two daughters: Lynette (Perreault) and LeAnn (Rezniecek).

Charles was engaged in dairy farming for 32 years but was involved in farming in some capacity his entire life. He and his wife purchased their own dairy farm in 1981 in Urness Township (section 5) on the corner of Douglas County roads 25 and 56. On October 31, 2001, they sold the dairy cows and continued to purchase Holstein feeder calves and raised them to finishing steers until Charles' unexpected death.

Charles took great pride in his cattle. Many times you could find him just walking amongst the herd admiring their nature. He valued family life and the family was active in the responsibilities of the farm work. Most evenings he liked to hop into his pickup and go around the block where he would maybe see a deer or two. But most importantly he would check the progress of his crops and see what the neighborhood folks had been up to. Besides farming, Charles enjoyed watching sporting events on television. His idea of great evening would be to make a big bowl of popcorn topped with melted butter on and sit down for an entertaining game of baseball, basketball, or football. He and his wife belonged to the couple's card club for over 25 years where they played 500. He also enjoyed hunting raccoons in his younger years and deer hunting" (bio and pictures submitted by Deb Plaster, Charles' wife).

Martin T. and Jennie Martin

Martin Theodore Martin was born November 9, 1907, and died May 8, 1995. "Martin's parents, Frank and Paulina Knopik, came to America from Poland. Martin, along with 14 siblings, grew up on a farm in Little Falls, MN.

When he was 22, he moved to Minneapolis to attend Business School.

While there, he met and married **Jennie Swenson**. They made their home in Minneapolis and raised seven children: Pauline (Jensen), Tony, Connie (Snider), Kathy (Stoddart), Dick, Michael and Adam. They had 21 grandchildren.

When Martin could find the time, he enjoyed playing the accordion— especially polkas!

Martin owned a successful auto repair shop (Martin Motors) in Minneapolis. However, his first love was farming, so in 1952 he bought the Albert Johnson farm and spent his weekends, pursuing his passion, farming.

Martin loved the farm. He was born on the farm. He was raised on the farm. He loved the work on the farm. It was hard for him to take a day of vacation. He never wanted his family to work on Sunday, 'a day of rest.' But every once in a while, you could catch him fixing something or taking a machine out into the field.

Although he was happiest when 'working in the field,' he appreciated the occasional rainy day so he could take off to go fishing.

Martin had a tender spot in his heart for animals. He would bring the chickens into the house to make pets of them, holding them and feeding them in the kitchen. The family dogs would always sit by him, knowing they wouldn't go away hungry.

Martin died at the age 87 from Non-Hodgkin's Lymphoma." (bio and picture contributed by daughter Kathy Stoddart)

Jennie L. Martin

"**Martin, Jennie L.** Age 100, died at home in Minneapolis Feb. 5. She was preceded in death by husband, Martin T. Martin; grandson, Robert Snider & great-grandson, Eric Skeie. She is survived by 4 sons & 3 daughters: Pauline Jensen, Anthony (Mary Ann), Constance Snider, Kathryn Stoddart (Russ), Richard (Kathleen), Michael (Valerie) & Allen; sister, Gladys Lawrence (Breckenridge, MN); 20 grandchildren & 9 great-grandchildren."(Published in Star Tribune on February 9, 2010)

"Jennie was born November 25, 1909, to **John and Mathilda Swenson** of Urness township, Douglas County, Minnesota. "Her siblings were **Helen Clow**, Alice Strand, Alden Swenson, and **Gladys Lawrence**. She attended grade school at the Evansville District no. 49, a one-room schoolhouse. She often mentioned being chased by Amundson's mad bull on the shortcut to and from school. She was always afraid because of the close calls when she 'barely made it under the fence.'

When her father butchered a cow, whe had to catch the blood which they mixed with flour and baked. Then they sliced and fried it...she said it was 'very good.'

Jennie and her sister **Helen** were 'pranksters.' Later in life, they loved to get together and giggle over their mischievous tricks. Jennie and her sisters loved to go dancing at Red Rock and Oakdale. They frequently bragged that their 'dance cards were always full.' Pa told them one Saturday night they couldn't go dancing, so they headed out in the opposite direction. When they were sure Pa was no longer watching, they sneaked back—only to be caught by Pa.

Her one regret was not being able to attend high school as Pa needed her for fieldwork on the farm.

While working as a waitress in Minneapolis, Jennie met and married Martin T. Martin. They made their home there and raised seven children: Pauline (Jensen), Tony, Connie (Snider), Kathy (Stoddart), Dick, Michael and Adam. They had 21 grandchildren.

Jennie's main interest was flowers. Her extensive gardens were admired by all. She also enjoyed needle work and completed many exquisite pictures. She loved pretty clothes and preferred bright colors in her attire. It was always fun to be around Jennie as she maintained her sense of humor and continued to joke with people up until her death at age 100." (bio and picture contributed by daughter Kathy Stoddart)

Anton and Karolina Nelson

Anton Nelson was born August 31, 1876, in Knared, Halland, Sweden,

to Nils Nilsson and Stina Svensdotter. He immigrated in 1899 at the age of 23. He married Catherina (**Karolina**)Larson, November 25 , 1903, in Fargo, North Dakota. They lived in Stutsman County, ND, where Lillian, Walter, and Hilvie were born. By 1911, they had taken up residence in Urness township, where Alphie, **Melford**, Arthur **Delmer**, and Arnold, **Kenneth** were born. (information and pictures from Selrock39 on ancestry.com) Their farm was the **Olof Alldrin** homestead.

Anton died September 18, 1967. (pictures also from Evansville Historical Foundation)

LtoR Lillian (Larson), Alphie (Noid), Shirley (Delmer's wife), Hilvie (Setterlund), Donna (Kenneth's wife) and Anton

Karolina "Carrie" Nelson

Carrie Larson Nelson was the daughter of Nels and Kerstin (Olsdotter) Larson born January 6, 1882 at Varmland Sweden. "At the age of 16 years, she immigrated to America, coming to her father's farm in Leaf Mountain, Otter Tail county. Upon residing there for three years, she moved to Fargo, No. Dak., to live with her sister, Mrs. Sam Edwards.

On Nov. 25, 1903, at Fargo, No. Dak., she was married to Anton Nelson...They operated a shoe store in Fargo for a short time. In the year 1905 they moved to Gackle, No. Dak., where they homesteaded for 5 years, moving to Urness township, Douglas county, in 1909 where they have resided ever since that time. They had seven children: Lillian (Arthur Larson,New Richmond, Wis.), **Walter**, Hilvie (Rudolph Setterlund, Alexandria), Alphie (Arthur Noid), **Milford (wife Mabel)**, Kenneth (wife

Donna living in California) and **Delmer (wife Shirley)**.

She was a member of Zionsborg since 1909 and active in church work, Ladies Aid and a life member of the Missionary Society." From *Park Region Echo*, December 23, 1954 On Nov. 25th, 1953, Carrie and Anton celebrated their golden wedding anniversary. Her funeral was December 19, 1954.

Delmer Nelson

According to Delmer's obituary, Delmer was the son of **Anton and Carrie (Larson) Nelson** and "was born August 31, 1916 in Douglas County. He was baptized and confirmed at Zionsborg. He served four and a half years in the Army during World War II, spending most of his time in the South Pacific (where he contracted malaria). He enlisted 16 Oct 1941 and was released 28 Aug 1945.

On November 15, 1947, he was united in marriage to Shirley J. Guthrie in Duluth. The couple farmed 240 acres in Elk Lake Township and retired from farming in 1972. Delmer enjoyed deer hunting, was a member of the Hoffman American Legion and a member of the VFW in Alexandria." (Douglas County Historical Society files)

His wife told us that she met Delmer up in Duluth when he was deer hunting and went to a local dance. On their wedding day, he went hunting in the morning and got married in the afternoon. He enjoyed saying he got two deer (dear) that day.

He had three brothers **Walter, Milford**, and Kenneth and three sisters Alphie Noid, Hilvie Setterlund and Lillian Larson. According to Shirley, he attended school district 49 and attended through 8th grade.

After marriage, They farmed on a farm by Elk Lake (the Harry Setterlund farm). In 1953 they moved to a farm on the county line and lived there until his death. Here they had milk cows and later beef cattle, geese, and chickens.

Milford and Mabel Nelson

"...**Milford Nelson**, was born September 12, 1913 in Urness Township, rural Evansville, to **Anton and Carolina (Larson) Nelson**. He was baptized in Zionsborg Lutheran Church, and confirmed in Immanuel Lutheran church both of Evansville. He grew up in Urness Township where he attended rural school. On June 29, 1941 he married **Mabel**. M. Thornberg in Minneapolis. From 1942 to 1946 he served in the U.S. Army during WWII in Germany and was involved in heavy artillery. Following his military service he returned to Urness Township and farmed. Mabel died May 8, 1989 and later that year he retired from farming. In 1990 he moved to Evansville and in 1993 entered the Crestview Manor Nursing Home.

He was a member of Lincoln Lutheran Church, rural Hoffman. He enjoyed league bowling, hunting, card playing and his special dog 'Smokey.'

He is survived by a brother Kenneth (Donna) Nelson of Riverside, CA; and many nieces and nephews. He was preceded in death by his parents, his wife, Mabel; Walter and **Delmer** and sisters, Lillian, Alphie and Helvie..." *Echo Press*, April 16, 2001.

He died at the age of 87, March 31, 2001 at Crestview Manor Nursing Home in Evansville.

Picture courtesy of Lincoln Lutheran Church archive

Mabel Meriam Nelson

Mabel Meriam Nelson was born February 6, 1913 to Nels and Anna Thornberg and grew up in Lund Township, Douglas County, Minnesota with six siblings: Oscar, Arthur, Magnus, George, Bertha , and Myrtle.

"She was united in marriage to **Milford Nelson** on June 29, 1941, and they lived in the Evansville community. She has been a member of the Lincoln Lutheran Church for twenty four years. Mabel died on May 8, 1989. Funeral services were Thursday, May 11, 1989, 2 p.m. at the Lincoln Lutheran church in [it is actually near] Hoffman, Minnesota with reverend Lloyd Nelson officiating. ..

Dorothy Schultz was organist and Elwood Nelson, soloist sang 'Just As I Am,' and 'What a Friend We Have in Jesus.' The congregational hymns were 'How Great Thou Art' and 'children of the Heavenly Father.'

Pallbearers were Darrell Grove, Walter Ostenson, Al Schultz, Kermit Zickur, Julian Olson and Kermit Fletcher..."*Lake Region Echo Press*, May 17, 1989.

Walter Nelson

His parents **Anton and Carrie** (Karolina)**Nelson** lived in Stutsman County, ND, where Lillian, Walter, and Hilvie were born.

Erick Nelson Home Page

Little is known of the home place for Erick and Marit Nelson. They immigrated to America in 1868 and moved to Erdahl township. According to the 1900 Erdahl Township plat map the Erick Nelson Estate was located in the western half of Section 25 consisting of 320 acres. Their son Alfred had 160 acres on the SE quarter of that Section.

Erick Nelson (Nilson)

Born 1840 in Sweden married **Marit** "Mary" Lindstrom had 1880 Census showed five children: **John**, Emily, Matilda, Alfred, and Hilma. He died in 1883. Nothing more known at this time.

Marit Nelson

(From the Lindstrom genealogy Evansville Historical Foundation) **Marit** was born in Sweden, February 17, 1843, in Varmland, Sweden, to John and Karin Jonsdotter (1802-1871)**Lindstrom**. Her siblings from this marriage included Lars, Gertrud and stepbrother Jon Persson. Marit married Erick Nilson December 29, 1867. They immigrated to America in 1868 and moved to Erdahl township.

The Evansville Enterprise reads, " Mrs. Mary Nelson died at her home in Erdahl on Saturday July 23, of cancer of the liver, after an illness of about five months. The funeral services were conducted by Rev. Holmer last Wednesday afternoon, and burial was made in the Zionsborg cemetery. She leaves five children to mourn for one who was always a kind and loving mother and a thorough Christian woman. The children are **John E. Nelson** and Miss Hilma Nelson, of Erdahl, Mrs. David Johnson and Miss Mathilda Nelson of Antler, N.D. , and Alfred E. Nelson, of Barnesville..."

John E. and Susie Nelson

Born to **Erick** and **Marit** (Lindstrom) **Nelson, John E.** was the first born upon his parents arrival to Minnesota in 1868. Not much is known about his childhood or young adulthood (See infant Nelson).

He married **Susie Alberts** November 17, 1910 at Evansville, Rev. C.E. Holmer officiating and moved to Elbow Lake. There he built a 50X60 brick garage with AJ Arneson and Ronald Nelson, he sold autos, farm equipment and did repairs. He was also one of the founders of Elbow Lake Oil Company. In 1924 he bought out Ed Gilbertson in the Elbow Lake Auto Corp. He died in 1944.

Susie Nelson

Susie (Albert)Nelson, the daughter of **Ole and Oline Alberts** was born in Evansville township on the Ole Alberts' homestead November 17, 1874. She married **John E. Nelson** November 17, 1910 at Evansville, Rev. C.E. Holmer officiating.

Her obituary in the *Grant County Herald* reads, "Mrs. John E. Nelson, a resident of Elbow Lake since 1911, passed away at her home Monday afternoon, August 21, 1939, at 5:15 o'clock. Her death was caused from creeping paralysis. Her feet and legs had been giving her trouble since January of this year but she got around by steadying herself on something or with the aid of her wheel chair until three weeks ago when she was confined to her bed...Mrs. Nelson was a member of the Swedish Lutheran church and of the ladies' aid. She was also a member of the Royal Neighbor and Eastern Star lodges.

She is survived by her husband, three brothers and one sister, namely, Adolph and Theodore Alberts of Elbow Lake, **Otto Alberts** of Los Angeles, Calif., and Mrs. George Gilbertson of Duluth, and eight nieces and nephews, **Denice**, Beulah, Irene and **Francis Alberts** of Urness township, Marion, Alton and Edmund Gilbertson of Duluth and Eugene Alberts of Elbow Lake..."

Unknown Infant Nelson

Very little is known about this infant. The caretaker's notes are "infant son of Johnny Nelson 1899-1900." *The Ashby News* August 23, 1900, reports that the one year old son of John E. Nelson died Sunday evening at 7:30. Is this the same child? Is this the same John E. Nelson who later married Susie Alberts? If so, who was he married to before? What happened to his first wife? Pete and Emma Nelson buried in the lot just west of this one lost a son in infancy but didn't live here until 1908. More questions than answers.

Peter Nelson

Born in Skone, Sweden May 2, 1855, Peter Nelson immigrated in 1881. He married Emma Lund August 29, 1892. For the first four years they made their home on a farm near Herman, and later lived for ten years in Delaware township. In 1908 they purchased a farm in Erdahl township. They had three boys: Adolph, John,and **Ernest** and five girls: Ella, Alma, Hilda, **Sigrid** and Esther(1910 Census). He died November 279, 1917.

Emma Nelson

Park Region Echo August 17, 1939 –"**Emma Lund Nelson** was born in Vastergotland, Sweden August 22, 1861. She was baptized and confirmed in the Lutheran faith in Sweden. She migrated to America at the age of 25 years. On August 29, 1892 she was united in marriage to **Pete H. Nelson** at Morris.

For the first four years they made their home on a farm near Herman, and later lived for ten years in Delaware township. In 1908 they purchased a farm in Erdahl township, where she has since made her home.

Mrs. Nelson is survived by seven children, namely: Adolph Nelson of Dilworth, Minn.; John R. Nelson of Evansville; Ella (Mrs. Arthur Johnson) of Holmes City; Alma (Mrs. Hjalmar Johnson) of Holmes City; Esther Ostlund of Evansville and Hilda and Ernest at home. She was preceded in death by her husband who passed away on May 18, 1939, and by a son who died in infancy. She is survived by 17 grandchildren.

She was a faithful member of the Zionsborg Lutheran church, and served as treasurer of its ladies aid for many years. She was a kind and loving mother, neighbor and friend, and will be greatly missed by all who knew her."

Not listed in this obituary is a daughter **Sigrid Dahlen** buried on the same lot.

Ernest Nelson

According to *The West Douglas County Record* February 24, 1983, obituary— "**Ernest V. Nelson** 86, of Erdahl died Thursday evening February 3rd at the Grant County Hospital in Elbow Lake...

The son of **Peter and Emma Nelson,** Ernest was born January 5, 1897 at Herman, MN. As a youngster the family moved to the Barrett area where they farmed for many years. Ernest worked for many families in the area as a hired man and in the 60's he worked as a painter. He had been a resident of rural Erdahl for several years.

He is survived by one sister, Mrs. Hilda Anderson of Minneapolis and several nieces and nephews. He was preceded in death by his parents, three brothers and four sisters.

John O. and Kathrina Peterson

According to the Farnell Family tree on Ancestry. Com., **John O Peterson** was born August 8,1822, in Asa, Kronosberg, Sweden , to Per Olofsson and Martha Jonasdotter. He was married to **Katharina** Svensdotter Nelson (according to the *History of Douglas and Grant County*) in Sweden. He immigrated in 1865 to Washington County. He settled and homesteaded in Elk Lake township where they homesteaded 160 acres. Here he farmed and raised stock until his death September 16,1887. He and his wife had six children: Marta, Mathilda, **Peter, Charles G., Frank A., and Martin**.

According to the *History of Douglas and Grant Counties*, "John O. and Katherine Peterson were prominent in the social and the church life of

the township and were among the organizers of the Zion [Zionsborg] Lutheran church. Mr. Peterson assisted in the building of the first school house in the township,which was also the first in the county. He had much to do with the civic life of the town-

93

ship and was for many years a member of the board of supervisors. He and his wife were parents of twelve children, Martha, Christine, Mary, Mathilda, John, **Peter J., Charles G, Frank A, Martin J.** and three who died in infancy."

Katrina Peterson

According to the Farnell Family tree on Ancestry. Com., Katrina was born August 10,1825, in Tolg, Kronosberg, Smoland, Sweden , to Sven Nilsson and Kjerstin Monsdotter. She was married to **John O. Peterson** in Sweden. They immigrated in 1865 to Washington County. Then they settled and homesteaded in Elk Lake township where they homesteaded 160 acres. Here he farmed and raised stock until his death September 16,1887. They had six children: Marta, Mathilda, **Peter, Charles G., Frank A., and Martin**.

Katrina died June 11, 1907.

Charles G. and Christianna Peterson

Charles Gustav Peterson was born in Sweden in 1865 and immigrated as a baby with his parents John O and Katrina Peterson in 1865. His siblings included , Christine, Mary, Mathilda, John, **Peter J., Frank A, Martin J.** and three who died in infancy . He married **Christianna** Erickson at Evansville on August 10, 1887 with Rev. Kronberg officiating.

They had seven children: **Capitola** (Albro, **Barron**), **Beatrice (Hickey)**, Carl, Cecil, **Vivian (Sowers), baby** Peterson, and **Euphemia**. He died in 1914.

Christianna Peterson

According to her obituary, **Christiana** was the daughter of Berger and Oline Erickson and born in Dane Prairie, Wisconsin, September 14, 1859. At age seven, she came with her parents to Dalton, Minnesota in a covered wagon. [Her siblings included Ole, Bernhardt, Cornelius, Otto, Karen, Anna, and Pauline.]

She married **Charles G. Peterson** at Evansville on August 10, 1887 with Rev. Kronberg officiating.They had seven children: **Capitola (Al-**

bro, **Barron**), Beatrice, Carl, Cecil, Vivian (Sowers), **baby Peterson, and Euphemia**.

When her husband died in 1914, she moved to Minneapolis to live with her daughter, Mrs. Vivian Sowers.

At the age of 95 she was a patient at the Fair View hospital and died July 25, 1954.

"Mrs. Peterson was endowed and blessed with a personality that radiated neighborliness, friendliness and kindness which surrounded her with a host of friends and the children knew her as "Grandma Peterson." She was laid to rest in the family lot in the Zionsborg cemetery.

Pallbearers were Franklin Peterson, John Sandberg, Palmer Bergerson, Raymond Peterson, Ben Leraas, and Selmer Peterson."

Baby Peterson and Euphemia Peterson

Euphemia was born in 1891 and died five months 12 days later. Her parents were **Charles and Christianna Peterson. Baby Peterson** was also born to Charles and Christianna.

Frank Peterson HomePage

PHOTO LEFT: This would have been the front entrance as the road came from the west. PHOTO RIGHT: This is the front entrance in 2012

Frank August was born January 16, 1867 in Washington County to John O. and Catherine Peterson. In 1868 he came to Grant with his parents.

"They lived in Erdahl township for three years, but moved back to the original homestead (see John O. Peterson) in Elk Lake, which was their home until they moved to Barrett in September, 1921. This farm is located in Elk Lake township sections 2 and 3.

Frank and Martha Peterson

Frank August was born January 16, 1867 in Washington County to John O. and Catherine Peterson. In 1868 he came to Grant with his parents. His siblings included Christine, Mary, Mathilda, Peter, Charles, and Martin. As a boy he attended school district No 1 in Elk Lake Township, which was the first established school in the county. According to the family history, he remembered the grasshopper plague as a small boy. Grasshoppers were so thick they cast a cloud over the sun, which they could not see because of the swarm. In desperation they tried to save some of their crops by spreading molasses on sheets.

January 29, 1889, he married **Martha** Thune at the William Olson home. Together they had six children: **Alfred, Martin, Franklin, Chester, Monroe**, and Alice (Ostrom).

"They lived in Erdahl township for three years, but moved back to the original homestead in Elk Lake, which was their home until they moved to Barrett in September, 1921. For several years Mr. Peterson was active in the management of the Barrett Oil company, disposing of his interest about a year ago. Mr. Peterson had a quiet, peaceable disposition, which coupled with his honesty and sincerity won him many friends. He has

always taken an active interest in the work of his church. He was a charter member of the Zionsborg Lutheran church and has always been one of its most faithful members serving as trustee for twenty-six years." (*Grant Co. Herald* May 27, 1926)

Frank Peterson died May 19, 1926 of stomach cancer.

Martha Peterson

Martha Thune was born February 2, 1870, in Vestre Toten, Oppland, Norway, to Peder and Margrete Thune. She had 8 siblings: Mathias, Maria, Johanna, Peder, Jens, Jorgine, Karen, and Julianna. She immigrated with her parents to America in 1882 and settled in Elk Lake township. She was baptized in Norway and confirmed in Minnesota, by Rev. Erdahl of the Lincoln Lutheran Church.

She married **Frank A. Peterson** in 1889. She and her husband were charter members of the Zionsborg Lutheran Church. Together they had seven children: **Alfred, Martin, Franklin, Chester, Monroe**, and Alice (Ostrom). She died of pneumonia August 3, 1962, at the age of 92. (information from Frank Peterson and her obituary)

Back Chester and Monroe. Front Alfred, Martin, and Franklin

Alfred and Olivia Peterson

(According to his obituary)Alfred was born June 30, 1893, in Elk Lake township to **Frank A. and Martha Peterson**; Alfred Peterson was one of six children: Chester, **Monroe, Alice, Martin**, Franklin, and himself. Alfred attended Northwestern college at Fergus Falls and Mankato Commercial College. During World War I, he was stationed at Camp Grant and attained the rank of Sargeant Major.

February 17, 1923, he and **Olive** Huseth were married in the Huseth home in Lien township and "for many years prominent in the business life of Barrett. He served as cashier of the Farmers State Bank of barrett, manager of the Barrett Oil Company, and took an active part in community...Following their residence at Barrett they spent a winter in Arizona and California for his health.

Some time before his death December, 10, 1932, he moved to Minneapolis and had recently been undergoing treatment at the Veteran's Hospital at Fort Snelling for asthma and pulmonary complications. Funeral services were held at Fridhem Church in Barrett. Military honors were accorded him by his comrades of Carlson-Sandberg post of the American Legion. Pall bearers were Harold Huseth, Carl Ostrom, Edwin Hegne, Victor Malmgren, John Johnson and Bennie Leraas. The Zionsborg choir sang "Abide With Me." Miss Ebba Anderson sang a solo with Rev. Constant Johnson. "The Great White Host" was sung by Rev. Carl A.E. Gustafson.

Alfred died at the age of 39, leaving a wife and daughter **Kathryn** 7. He was survived by one sister Alice (Mrs. C.V.Ostrom) of Evansville and three brothers Martin and Franklin of Barrett and Chester of Starbuck. (Grant County Historical Society obits and Frank Peterson)

Olivia Peterson

Olivia or Olive Peterson was born August 28, 1895, to Eric and Signe Huseth. Her siblings were Oswald, Harold, Josie, Selmer, Clarence, and Norma. February 17,1923, she married **Alfred Peterson in Lien township. Olivia was a school teacher**.

The 1930 census shows her living in La Crescenta, Los Angeles, California, with Alfred, daughter **Kathryn (later Domas)**, Alfred's sister Alice, and Olive's father Eric.

(Arnold) Monroe Peterson

Chester and Monroe

98

Arnold Monroe Peterson was born in Elk Lake township March 18, 1903, to **Frank A. and Martha** Peterson. Better known as Monroe, he was one of six siblings: **Alfred, Martin, Franklin**, Chester, Alice and himself.

Monroe attended college at Northwestern College in Fergus Falls. He was ill only about a week, was taken to a hospital and had benefit "of the best medical skill, but his life could not be saved." He died of burst appendicitis. He was a little less than 16 years old and described as a bright, patient, obedient youth with a happy disposition.

"The funeral was held at the home and at Zionsborg Lutheran church. Rev. Oscar O. Gustafson of elbow Lake preached the funeral sermon, and Professor Yngve of Northwest also spoke words of comfort and cheer and told about Monroe's record as a student. Two of his school mates sang "There' Be No Parting" and "Nearer My God to Thee." Miss Pearson, teacher of voice at the college sang very beautifully "Det Brister en Streng..." [perhaps "There is a lack of Strength"

Six young friends from Elk Lake and Northwestern were pall bearers. (information from Grant County Historical Society obits and Frank Peterson)

Marten Peterson

Marten Peterson was the son of **John O. and Katrina Peterson** and was born 1869 and died 1890. *The Herman Enterprise* "Died, on Tuesday, March 18 1890, of consumption, Martin Peterson, in the twenty-second year of his age. Mr. Peterson was a brother-in-law of John G. Peterson and James E. Williams of this county."

Martha Jean Peterson

Martha Jean was born November 28, 1931, to Franklin and Myrtle Peterson but only lived three days. She died December 1, 1931 and is buried on her grandparents' **Frank and Martha Peterson's** burial lot.

99

Peter J. and Karen Peterson

Born December of 1862 in Sweden to **John O. and Katrina Peterson** and immigrated with his family in 1865.

He married **Karen** Thune, sister to **Martha**, who married Peter J.'s brother **Frank** December 29, 1889. Their children included Mathilda Cerine (Okerlund), Stella (Dean), **Maranda**, Johan, Alma, Carron,and Carl.

He and his wife were charter members of Zionsborg. He died in July 8, 1921.

Karen Peterson

"The funeral for Mrs. Karen Matea Peterson formerly of Elk Lake township of Grant County was held at the Zionsborg church October 8 at 2:00. Rev. Erni T. Holm of Evansville officiated. Rev. Ivar Sandberg of Barrett spoke. Mrs. Carron Peterson of Minneapolis and Preus Frykman sang solos.

"Karen Matea Thune Peterson was born in Norway, August 11, 1868. She came to America with her parents in 1882. She was united in marriage to Peter J. Peterson of Elk Lake township on December 29, 1889. They made their home about six miles from Barrett.

"Mr. and Mrs. Peterson were the parents of seven children...Mrs. Peterson has not been in this community for the past forty years. She passed away at the Willmar State Hospital on October 3, at the age of 79..." (*Grant Co. Herald* 1947)

John P. Peterson

"Johan Preus Peterson died at the home of his parents, **P.J.** Peterson in Elk Lake township on Friday evening May 7th. Deceased suffered from Spinal Meningitis and had been sick for a period of about three weeks before death claimed him. He was born September 8th, 1896, at his home, and had spent his young and happy days helping his father with the farm work. He had a good education and he left many friends who mourn his departure...The deceased's cousins acted as pallbearers..." (*Grant County Herald*, May 20, 1915)

Marande Peterson

Marande E. Peterson was born October 30, 1894 in Elk Lake township **to Peter J. and Karen Peterson**. She was one of seven children: Mathilda Cerine, Stella, Marande, Johan (John Preus), Alma, Carron, and Carl. (information from Frank Peterson) The 1900 census shows Mathilda, Stella, John P, Maranda, and Alma- Marande never married and was a school teacher. She died March 13, 1917. (Information from Frank Peterson) *The Alex Post* noted that she was sick for the last three years of her life suffering with tuberculosis.

Kenneth A Peterson

Kenneth A Peterson was born to Emil and Gertrude (Nelson) Peterson (Gertrude was a sister of **Esther Hanson**) June 17, 1925 (probably Huron, Beadle, South Dakota.) He had a brother Robert and a sister Delores.

We know he enlisted in the armed forces September 15, 1943, and was released January 28, 1946.

According to the US social Security Death Index his last residence was Stillwater, Washington County, Minnesota, when he died September 23, 1987.

The Hoffman Tribune, October 1, 1987, "...As a young man he moved with the family to Stillwater where he continued his education.

"Mr. Peterson served in the South Pacific during World War II, and after serving his country he worked as an auto mechanic and for many years as a bartender. On his retirement, Kenneth came to Hoffman to live, and most recently has made his home in the Hofman Care Center in Hoffman. He was a member of the Huron American Legion Post where he had also been a Junior Member of the Drum Corp.

"Kenneth A Peterson, age 62, of Hoffman, MN, passed away on Wednesday, Sept. 23, 1987, at the Hoffman Care Center..."

Peter and Emilia Peterson

Peter "Pit" Peterson was born in Sweden November 3, 1851. He emigrated from Sweden in 1868, according to the US Census reports. Although the 1900 census reports that he immigrated in 1861 when he was ten, all the other censuses indicated the 1868 immigration date. He was married November 28, 1880, to **Emilia Erickson**. They made their home in Elk Lake township where they engaged in farming. They had seven children who lived to adulthood: John, Hilma, Amanda, Alma, Ellen, and Florence (The five infants, who died between 1880 and 1905 are buried in Zionsborg on their lot and are listed as **A.V.P, C.B.P, C.J.P., A.J.P, and C.B.P.** However, we may have found six buried on their lot. See their page for more information.)

Peter Peterson was a charter member of the Zionsborg Lutheran Church joining in (Dec. 19) 1884. In 1930 he lived in Minneapolis, with his daughter Florence Sandberg and family and died November 6, 1936, at the age of 85.

Emilia Peterson

The headstone reads "(Mother 1862-1924)"

According to the obituaries in the *Elbow Lake Tribune*, **Emelie (Erickson)Peterson** was born in September 14, 1862 in Wisconsin to Jacob and Maren (Hansdotter)Erickson the daughter of Norwegian immigrants .

"She lived in Decorah, Iowa, and later in Fillmore county, Minnesota. In April of 1880, she came to Grant County." She was married November 28, 1880, to **Peter "Pit" Peterson**, who emigrated from Sweden in 1868, according to the US Census reports. "They made their home in Elk Lake township where Mr. Peterson engaged in farming. From the time of the marriage until the time of her death, forty-four years, Mrs. Peterson has lived on the farm in Elk Lake."

Mrs. Peterson was a charter member of the Zionsborg Lutheran Church joining in (Dec. 19) 1884. Funeral services were held at the church Tuesday, September 3oth...there was a large gathering from far and near was present to pay their last respects to the deceased woman. Rev. Johnson said of her, 'Mrs. Peterson was a true Christian, an esteemed neighbor and a faithful member of the church.' Interment was made in the church cemetery. The pall bearers were **Oscar Malmgren, Frank Peterson**, Gunder Jenstad, August Peterson, **John N. Frykman and John P. Frykman.**

Mrs. Peterson is survived by her husband, Peter Peterson, and by six daughters and one son: Mrs. John Lindquist, Cambridge; Mrs. Albert Erickson, Barrett; Mrs. Fred Westerberg, Minneapolis, Mrs. Emil Nelson, Wolf Point, Mont., **John** and Ellen Peterson at home, and Mrs. Carl Sandberg, Barrett..."

Two sisters and five children preceded Mrs. Peterson in death."

A.V.P, C.P.P, C.J.P., A.J.P, and C.B.P

Six infant children of **Peter 'Pit' and Emelia Peterson** are buried but not all marked. Some are unknown names and dates at this time. It was thought there were only 5, but in 2012, an additional unmarked infant burial was found on the lot. The Grant County death index has an Amanda J. died March 7, 1889, at one year and 10 months and another Amanda died July 25, 1890 10 months 10 days and a **Claus P.** born December 25, 1899 and died February 10, 1900 of Whooping cough. All of these are recorded as children of Peter and Emelia Peterson. According to the 1900 census, Emelia and Pit had 10 children of which five were living. Included in the census was **John**, Martha, Alma, Hilvie, Manda, and Edna (possibly Ellen). In 1905 Alice is born and is listed on the 1905 census as 8 months old, but not listed in any more census, therefore, possibly the AVP – Alice Victoria.

John B. Peterson

John B Peterson was born in August 14, 1881 to **Peter "Pit" and Emelia (Erickson) Peterson** in Elk Lake Township, Grant County. He had six sisters that survived infancy: Martha, Hilma, Alma, Amanda, Ellen and Florence. The six infants, who died between 1880 and 1905 are buried in Zionsborg and are listed as **A.V.P, C.B.P, C.J.P., A.J.P, and C.B.P.** He grew up in this community, attended rural school and was confirmed in the Zionsborg Church.

He lived in Fort Peck Reservation, Roosevelt County, Montana in 1930 with his brother-in-law Emil Nelson and Ervin Nelson. He was employed in Minneapolis and after the death of his wife he made his home with his sister Ellen. He died February 4, 1958 Hennepin County, Minneapolis.

His obituary in the *Park Region Echo* Feb 20, 1958, reads, "Services for John B. Peterson were held Friday, Feb. 7, at 7:30 p.m. from the Henry W. Anderson mortuary in Minneapolis and at 1 p.m. Saturday, Feb. 8, at the Zionsborg Lutheran church. Pastor Harold Manson officiated.

Preus Frykman sang "I'm A Stranger" and "There's A Land That is fairer Than Day", accompanied by Mrs. Oliver Fedje. Pallbearers were Prues Frykman Alvin Frykman, Martin Peterson, Franklin Peterson, Maynard Larson and Robert Lindstrom... Survivors include four sisters: Mrs. Amanda Nelson of Wolf Point, Mont., Mrs. Hilma Erickson, Mrs, Charles Strafelda and Mrs. Carl Sandberg of Minneapolis."

John E., Mathilda, and John E. Petterson

Little is known of these three: John E 1888-1889, **Mathilda** 1886-1886, and **John E.** 1891-1891. The last name Petterson was used on the headstone. According to the Grant Co. Death Records, a John E Petterson, 1891 died Oct 4- 15 days old; Christina (not Mathilda) died Oct 14 1886; and John E born 1888 died March 1889, 5 months 25 days- died of lung fever, all children of Ole and Ida. They may be the children of Ole B. and Ida Peterson of Elk Lake township. Ole was the son of John G. and Helena Peterson. Ole and Ida were married in 1884. The 1900 census shows that they had 10 children with only 3 living—Josephina 15, Maria 12, and Effie 10. Later they had a son, Vincent. If these are their three children, where are the other four children buried? And why bury them in Zionsborg, when Ole lived near Elk Lake, very close to Lincoln Church and cemetery and there is a pioneer cemetery nearby?

The two boys match names and dates, and the girl matches dates but not name. John O and Katrina buried in the next lot lost 3 children in infancy. But I found no evidence that these three are theirs.

Robert Roe

Robert L. Roe, Jr., was born October 29, 1958, in Minneapolis to Robert, Sr., and **Joan (Borgen) Roe**. His grandparents were **Helmer and Pearl Borgen** and great-grandparents were **August and Julia (Annie) Borgen**.

Rob lived a rich and varied life, albeit short. He was employed by the Minneapolis Star and Tribune, where he won numerous awards and trips for sales. Later he moved on to Tele-communication Sales, in Nebraska, Oklahoma, Kansas, Washington, Idaho, Oregon, Nevada, Georgia, and Minnesota. He enjoyed writing including poetry. He wrote:
"Love that is shared is a beautiful thing
For that will make our hearts sing."

Picture and story contributed by Joan Roe.

Edwin Rohloff

Edwin Rohloff was born April 21, 1917 on a farm south of Evansville to Julius "Jules" and Alma Rohloff. He was the eldest of six children: Edwin, Ethel, Carl, Teddy, Marian, and Roseann.

He married Gladys Erickson daughter of Ludwig and Alma in Immanuel Lutheran church in Evansville, on June 1, 1941. Her attendant was Marion Rohloff and Kenneth Erickson was best man. The reception was held at Gladys's parents home. And the shivaree was at Jule Rohoffs' that evening and a wedding dance in the Erdahl hall.

According to Gladys, "there were many pleasant and fun times for the year 1941 until May 1942 when the US Army drafted Edwin. He left for Minneapolis and then to Mississippi. Other than furlougs, Edwin and Gladys did not see each other until Edwin's service ended. Edwin suffered from hernia for which he had surgery, malaria, and hepatitis.

Edwin and Gladys had four daughters: Lavonna "Vonnie" 1946, Eileen (Martin-Peterson)1951, Colleen (Marshall) 1957, and Rhonda (Hjelle)1959.

He worked for the county highway department and Johnson Grain as manager before he died of heart failure April 3, 1970.

Children L to R: Rhonda, Lavonna, Colleen and Eileen

Peter Setterlund Home Page

(From the Grant County Historical Setterlund file) "Peter Setterlund and family first came and settled on some land in Erdahl Township just across the township line from the farm where they later built another set of buildings. In the spring of 1883, they constructed a dugout into the side of a hill. It had a cellar dug into the hill behind it also in which to store potatoes and other vegetables. The dugout faced southwest, and its windows were on that side. Peter and

Kari Setterlund brought seven children along with them from Sweden, and three children Oscar, Victor and Emma were born in this dugout. Because this building was small to house a family that large, triple bunk beds were used. The land on which the family originally settled, an eight acre tract, was state land.

By 1888 Peter Setterlund had acquired additional land in Elk Lake Township, and built first a basement. The east side of the present Setterlund house formed this original house. The eight acres on which this second home was built was railroad land when purchased, and together with two forties which were school land, combined with the original eight acres in Erdahl Township comprised their 240 acre farm."

Peter and Karin Setterlund

Peter Setterlund was born December 27, 1844, in Torsby, Varmland, Sweden, to Peter Olsson and Karin Mattsdotter. (As tradition held, his name was Peter Peterson, but when he came to Barrett there was already a Peter Peterson so he took the name Setterlund.) He married **Karin** Johnsdotter November 1, 1868. They immigrated to America in 1883 and moved to the Barrett area in 1884.They had ten children Anna (Betty), Marie (Mary), Johan August, Nils (Nels), Karl (Carl or Charles), Olof (Ole), Anders (Benny), Oscar, **Emma** (who later married **Oliver Fedje**), and **Axel Victor.**

"In Sweden he had been a sailor, had become used to the handling of steam engines...so it was quite natural that he should become the engineer on one of the old steam threshing rigs used at the time. An engineers certificate issued by the state of Minnesota to Peter Setterlund in 1884 is among the Setterlund keepsakes." In addition, he was an excellent blacksmith, ox driver, and acted as the community dentist (*History of Grant County*)

Peter "was a charter member of Zionsborg as well as an active mem-

ber and officer. He was a charter member of the Northwestern College Corporation of Fergus Falls. He took an active part in the affairs of the township and the county and served as supervisor in Elk Lake township for several years.

He was a man of great strength and an iron constitution." (*Grant County Herald obituary*) Peter died February, 16, 1927. (Picture from the Grant Co. Historical Society)

Karin Setterlund

Karin Setterlund was born January 16, 1840, in Varmland Sweden to Jonas Petterson and Kerstin Larsdotter. Her sister was Mrs. **Clara (Nels J.) Frykman**.

She married **Peter Setterlund** November 1, 1868. They immigrated to America in 1883, him in the spring and her in the fall with seven of their children. (From the *Evansville Enterprise* obituary) "With her were also their seven children, which, of course, made her voyage not an easy one. Later three more children were born to this home...Since 1884 she has been a member of the Zionsborg congregation...It was her pleasure to partake in the church work and to her it was not burdensome...One thing we remember Mrs. Setterlund by especially, was the hyms she had committed to her memory. These she used freely. It was a joy to hear her repeat the Swedish psalms." They had ten children Anna (Betty), Marie (Mary), Johan August, Nils (Nels), Karl (Carl or Charles), Olof (Ole), Anders Benny), Oscar, **Emma** (who later married **Oliver Fedje**), and **Axel Victor**. She died September 24, 1930, at the age of 90.

August Setterlund

August Setterlund was born John August on July 11, 1873, to Peter (Peterson) and Karin Setterlund in Torsby, Varmland, Sweden.

He immigrated with his parents to America in

108

1883 and moved to the Barrett area in 1884.

(*History of Grant County*) He lived on nearby farms most of his life. He married a daughter of Halver Anderson, one of the very early settlers of the township. They had three children Cora (Glen Kasten), Rudolph, and Harry.

According to a family tree on Ancestry.com [Selrock] Johan August Setterlund married Hilda Teoline Anderson April 3, 1903, in Elk Lake, Grant County, MN. His wife is buried in Lincoln Lutheran Cemetery.

Axel Victor Setterlund

Axel, better known as Victor, was born February 2, 1888, last of the Setterlund children. "Victor became popular for his carvings of people and animals. He never married but remained on the home farm until his death. He was considered ingenius and definitely eccentric. He carved a 'fake runestone' which is on display at the Grant County Museum at Elbow Lake. " (Zionsborg History notes) He died June 2, 1976. picture by Bill Bank courtesy Grant Co. Historical

Solberg Home Page

As it looks in 2012, The center part was probably the original and the two side wings and porches added on

Lake Solberg, looking east from the house

The 1870 census showed that Abraham H. Solberg owned land in Evansville township. The 1878 land office showed he registered his homestead as Evansville township in sections 30 and 31. He also owned a strip of land in Sec. 36 of Erdahl township, Grant county adjacent to the road (County Road 54)by his farm. There was a cattle pass put in under the road by either Solbergs or later by Leonard Dahlen.

Abraham Hanson Solberg and Karen Solberg

Not much is known about **Abraham Hanson Solberg**. But this seems to be the hard-luck family. He and his wife had eight children, only Anna married (Henryk Johnson)and had children. A number of their children die as young adults. Two of their daughters die in their 20's from consumption, one son of appendicitis at the age of 19, and another daughter in her 40's.

Abraham was born February 10, 1837, in Norway. One World Family Tree researcher has his parents listed as Hans and Ingen Solberg. He married his wife Karen March 24, 1868 and immigrated to America in 1868. The 1880 census shows he is 43 and **Karen** his wife is 33. They have five children: **Selma, Hanna, Hans, Otto, and Gina** all born in Minnesota. By 1885 they have added, **Adolph** to the family and Anna in 1889. And in 1890 they have Johan **William**. All, except Anna, are buried at Zionsborg in the family lot and on the adjacent lot of Forsberg.

Abraham died in 1894 at the age of only 57. He had a daughter who died in 1893 from consumption and another that died in 1903. Consumption or tuberculosis was very contagious and this was prior to vaccinations.

Karen Solberg

Karen was born December 19, 1846 in Ringerike, Norway to Ole and Martha Fagre according to a One World researcher She married Abraham Hanson Solberg March 24, 1868 and immigrated to America in the spring of 1868. They had eight children: **Selma, Hanna, Hans, Otto, Gina, Adolph**, Anna (Johnson), and Johan **William**, all born in Urness township, Douglas County, Minnesota. All, except Anna, are buried at Zionsborg in the family lot and on adjacent lots of Forsberg and Franzen.

She had one brother, Hans Fagre of Wendell. "Mrs. Karen Solberg was one of the pioneer mothers in this community. She was a 'patient sufferer and had been unable to be out and about for several years. For some time she had been unable to see with her physical eyes, but she could see clearly with the eyes of faith, that which is of the greatest value to every individual. She was a good mother and kind neighbor and true friend'" (from her obituary *Evansville Enterprise*). Her daughter Anna married Henry Johnson and had four children, Delores, Arnold, Verne, and Beverly.

Karen died November 8, 1937.

Adolph Solberg

Adolph was born 27 Mar 1881 in Urness township, Douglas County, Minnesota to **Abraham Hanson and Karen (Fagre)Solberg**. He died in May 9, 1958.

Gina Thorim Solberg

Gina Thorim Solberg was born March 1, 1879, in Evansville Township to **Abraham and Karen** (Fagre) Solberg. However, at the young age of 24 she died at home of consumption on March 19, 1903. The *Evansville Enterprise*, March 27, 1903, stated, "She leaves behind a mother, two sisters and three brothers to mourn the loss of one who was dear to them. Miss Solberg was a favorite among her acquaintances and a large circle of sorrowing friends extend their sympathy to those who have lost a dear one.

The place in the home that no other can fill is vacant, and the memory, of a loving daughter and sister is one that will remain with them as long as life lasts." The funeral was held at Zionsborg church with Reverend T.A. Sattre officiating.

Hannah Solberg

Hannah Solberg was born August 18, 1870, in Evansville Township to **Abraham and Karen** (Fagre) Solberg. However, at the young age of 23 she died at home of consumption. The *Evansville Enterprise* August 4, 1893, stated, "Miss Hanna Solberg , daughter of Mr. and Mrs. Abraham Solberg passed quietly away from this life on July 29th, of the residence of her parent in Evansville township. The deceased has been a sufferer from consumption the past three years, and which was the result of her death. She was born in this township on Aug. 18th 1873 where she resided ever since. She leaves, besides parents, four brothers and three sisters to mourn her death, together with a host of friends and acquaintances. The family took place from [sic] her home on Tuesday at 3 o'clock. A large concourse of friends witnessed the last sad ceremonies and interment of the dead at Zion Borg [sic] cemetery. Rev. Sattre delivered the funeral sermon and paid a fitting tribute to a loving daughter and sister."

Hans Solberg

According to the *Evansville Enterprise* April 24, 1896, "Last Saturday morning at 2 o'clock Hans Solberg of the town of Erdahl, Grant county, died of a appendicitis, after being sick only about one week. Dr. Ward, of Evansville, was called to see him about four days before his death, and at once told him his only safety was in an operation to remove the pus that was collecting in the bowels, and that unless an operation was performed the abcess would break in a very few days, and he would be taken with a chill and die in a few hours. Mr. Solberg was a strong young man and could not believe that he was so near death's door, and would not consent to have an operation performed, until Friday night, when he had become convinced that is was his only hope. Dr. Ward at once sent to Alexandria for assistance, as one physician cannot perform the operation, and Dr. McEwan promptly responded, but before the physicians could get out there the patient had died. The abcess [sic] broke about 7:30 o'clock Friday night, and Mr. Solberg was taken with a chill and died at 2 o'clock the next morning. This should be a warning to others not to hesitate too long when their physician says the only hope is in an operation. Mr.Solberg was a strong, healthy young man and up to his last illness scarcely knew what it was to be sick. He was liked by a large circle of acquaintances, and every one sympathizes with his family in their bereavement." **Hans** was born to **Abraham and Karen (Fegre) Solberg** August 2, 1872. He was only 24 when he died.

Otto Solberg

Otto A. Solberg was born June 12, 1875 in Urness township, Douglas County, Minnesota to **Abraham Hanson and Karen (Fagre) Solberg**. He died August31,1944.

Selma Solberg

According to the *Park Region Echo* July 16, 1914, "**Selma Solberg** beloved daughter of **Mrs. Abraham Solberg** passed away at the Swedish hospital, Minneapolis, Sunday morning after a lingering illness. Deceased was aged forty five years and was well known having grown to womanhood on the farm in the vicinity of Evansville. About two and one half years ago Miss Solberg suffered an attack of rheumatism and a number of complications set in afterwards. The best of care was given her and many treatments tried but it seemed that it was of no help. During all her suffering she was patient and hopeful and when her sister Anna left her a week ago at the hospital she was much improved and expected to come home later. Somehow she was exposed and contracted a cold from which she did not recover. Miss Anna Soberg [sic] and her brother **William** left for Minneapolis on the night train to bring the remains home for burial which occurred Thursday in the cemetery of the Swedish Luth. Church near the home ..." Selma was born August 23, 1868 to **Abraham and Karen (Fagre) Solberg**.

William Solberg

Johan William born 6 Feb 1886 in in Urness township, Douglas County, Minnesota to **Abraham Hanson and Karen (Fagre)Solberg**. He died in January 28, 1954.

Vivian Sowers

Vivian Sowers was the daughter of **Charles and Christiana Peterson** and was born May 26, 1896 in Barrett. She worked as a beautician for many years in the Twin Cities area. She died September 25, 1978 at the Crystal Care Center in Minneapolis.

At the time of her death she was survived by a neice Dorothy Aspelin, Minnetonka, MN, and nephew Warren Peterson, Billings MT. (*Grant County Herald* September 28, 1978.

John Swenson Home Page

Picture from Kathy Stoddard- John with Alden on his lap, Mathilda with Alice, and Jennie and Helen in front of the house.

Immigrating in 1892, John Swenson began his citizenship life in America as a hired man. According to his granddaughter Sharon Kalland, John and his brother had their passage paid by a farmer in North Dakota. The 1900 census shows he lived with **John and Ellen Johnson**, as a boarder, age 33. Sometime between 1892 and 1900, John homesteaded in Urness township on Range 40 section 6 on 80 acres, which "he bought for $1200. The first year he built two rooms, a bedroom and a lving room. The second year he built a kitchen. The house was built almost entirely by John, including all plastering and carpentry work. He spent only forty dollars for work on the house that was done by other men." (from Kathy Stoddart) Alice Strand, daughter of John and Mathilda, remembered lightning hitting the house or bed her brother was sleeping in, and he got a burn impression of the springs on his back.

John was instrumental in establishing the Zionsborg Church.

John and Mathilda Swenson

John Swenson was born in Knared, Sweden, February 17, 1867. He and his brother immigrated to America in 1892. According to an article in the Evansville Historical Foundation files, "John came to America in 1892 worked as a hired hand for a few years went back to Sweden but came back to America. He came from a very poor family, also. There were times that tree bark was ground and added to the flour to be used in making bread." In 1900, he lived with John and Ellen Johnson .

He married **Mathilda Lindstrom**, daughter of Lars and Marie Lindstrom of Urness , December 26, 1905. They had five children—**Helen (Merrit Clow)**, Alice (Hugo Strand), Alden (Mildred Clow), **Jennie (Martin T. Martin)**, and **Gladys (Chas. Lawrence)**. (Information found at the Evansville Historical Foundation.)

They lived on the homeplace until 1941, when they moved into Evansville. Mathilda died October 2, 1943 of cancer. John lived with his daughter Helen's family for many years during the Spring through fall, and Jennie's family during the winter. His granddaughter Sharon Kalland has great memories of him and felt he was a great inspiration to her for his strong faith. She remembers him reading his Swedish Bible every day. John died March 8, 1961, at the age of 94.

Seated in Zionsborg Church Helen, Sharon, and Merrit Clow and John Swenson

Mathilda Swenson

Mathilda Swenson was born in the town of Urness November 21, 1874, to Lars and Marie (Bredsberg) Lindstrom. She had five sisters, Carolina (Erickson), Mary, Emma, Manda, Jenny, and Hulda (Decker) and three brothers John, Nils, and Oscar. She was baptized and confirmed in Fryksande Church.

"Times were hard and they lived a frugal existence. At one time, the family didn't have anything to eat. Lars walked to Holmes City, got a sack of flour and carried it home on his back. After returning home, a meal of mush was cooked so the family could eat." (Evansville Historical Foundation file)

According to the family history by Carolyn Townsend, Mathilda's father died at the age of 54 of stomach cancer, leaving her mother to raise 10 children on her own. Her mother died in 1903. Tillie must have moved in with Caroline, her sister, and Gust Erickson, for the 1905 census shows her living there. There is a story that Tillie (Mathilda) and a man named Gustaf were in love and had exchanged letters. However, his mother intercepted them and both believed the other was no longer interested.

She married **John Swenson** December 26, 1905. They had five children—**Helen (Merrit Clow)**, Alice (Hugo Strand), Alden (Mildred Clow), **Jennie (Martin T. Martin)**, and **Gladys** (Chas. Lawrence). Again according to the family history, it seems neither John nor Tillie were romantics. They hung their wedding pictures in an unprotected corn crib and let their children play with their wedding clothes.

Tillie and her sister Caroline remained "close both geographically and emotionally, and would often walk across fields—with little children—to visit one another. Their families always celebrated Christmas together."

"Tillie had beautiful auburn hair that she wore in a French knot. She was graceful and artistic. She crocheted, made beautiful rugs, and carved horses, and did many of these things from memory after seeing something she admired." Family members also remember her wonderful Angel Food cakes.

John and Matilda Swenson

They lived on the homeplace until 1941, when they moved into Evansville. Mathilda died October 2, 1943, of colon cancer. John died March 8, 1961, at the age of 94. (Information found at the Evansville Historical Foundation.)

Lars Westling

LARS
1827 — 1917

KERSTI
1825 — 1910

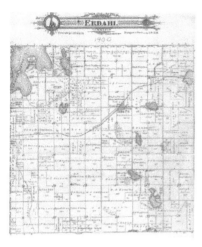

May 1827, Lars Westling was born in Sweden (most likely Fryksande, Varmland, Sweden) and immigrated to the United States 1888 with his wife and two sons, Lars, Jr. and Gustaf. It is unknown if that is his surname since so many people changed their names upon arrival to America. They settled on a farm in section 33 of Erdahl township, Grant Co. He died in 1917. He was a cousin to Peter Alldrin, one of the charter members of Zionsborg.

Kersti Westling

Kersti Westling was born born in Sweden (most likely Fryksande, Varmland, Sweden) September 20, 1825 to Per and Kersti Jonson. She married Lars in 1861 and in 1888 they immigrated to America with their two adult sons Lars, Jr., and Gustaf. According to the census these were the only children of Kersti and Lars, Sr. They made their home in Erdahl township. Lars, Jr., married and had at least one child Alma (Berg) and he died in Saskatchewan, Canada, where he lived with his daughter. Gustaf remained single and on the farm until his death in 1942. Kersti died May 8, 1910, of a cerebral hemorrhage.

Gustaf Westling

Gustaf Westling was born in Fryksande, Varmland, Sweden November 21, 1866, to **Lars and Kerstin Westling.** He immigrated to America with his parents and brother Lars Jr., in 1888. They settled in Erdahl township, Grant County, where he made his home until his death in 1942 According-ing to the *Grant County Herald*, Gustaf had become blind sixteen years prior to his death and for the last twelve years he lived alone and did his own housekeeping and cooking. A few weeks before his death he became ill and was taken to the Douglas County hospital where he died. At his death he had a nephew Anton Westling and a niece, Mrs. Alma Berg, in Canada, a cousin Peter Alldrin, address unknown and another cousin in Montana.

CPSIA information can be obtained at www.ICGtesting.com
Printed in the USA
BVOW11s1707060914

365716BV00008B/12/P